ASSIST
OUR SONG

Published by
The Bible Reading Fellowship
First Floor, Elsfield Hall
15–17 Elsfield Way, Oxford OX2 8FG
Website: www.brf.org.uk

ISBN-10 1 84101 446 X
ISBN-13 978 1 84101 446 3

First published 2006
10 9 8 7 6 5 4 3 2 1 0

Acknowledgments

Unless otherwise stated, scripture quotations are taken from The New Revised
Standard Version of the Bible, Anglicized Edition, copyright © 1989, 1995 by the
Division of Christian Education of the National Council of the Churches of Christ in
the USA, and are used by permission. All rights reserved.

Scripture quotations from The Revised Standard Version of the Bible, copyright ©
1973, 1978, 1984 by International Bible Society. Used by permission of Hodder &
Stoughton Ltd. All rights reserved. 'NIV' is a registered trademark of International
Bible Society. UK trademark number 1448790.

Scripture quotations taken from the Holy Bible, New International Version, copyright
© 1946, 1952, 1971, Apocrypha copyright © 1957, by the Division of Christian
Education of the National Council of the Churches of Christ in the United States of
America, are used by permission. All rights reserved.

The Collect for Michael and All Angels from *Common Worship: Services and Prayers for
the Church of England* is copyright © The Archbishops' Council 2000 and is
reproduced by permission.

The Sanctus and Gloria as they appear in *Common Worship: Services and Prayers for the
Church of England* (Church House Publishing, 2000) are copyright © The English
Language Liturgical Consultation and are reproduced by permission of the publisher.

The Viktorus Petkus prayer from Lithuania is copyright © Keston Institute,
38 St Aldates, Oxford OX1 1BN, and is used by kind permission.

A catalogue record for this book is available from the British Library

Printed in Singapore by Craft Print International Ltd

ASSIST
OUR SONG

Angels then and now

CAROL HATHORNE

For my husband, Mark

ACKNOWLEDGMENTS

*I should like to thank all the people who have been prepared
to share their most personal and precious spiritual
experiences with me. I am grateful to Naomi Starkey and all
at BRF for giving me the opportunity to write this book.
I should also like to thank my family and friends for their
unfailing love and support.*

*All names have been changed, except when people have
specifically asked to retain their own.*

CONTENTS

Ye holy angels bright,
Who wait at God's right hand,
Or through the realms of light
Fly at your Lord's command,
Assist our song,
Or else the theme
Too high doth seem
For mortal tongue.

RICHARD BAXTER (1651–91)

❖

INTRODUCTION

We knocked the man down on Boxing Day 1999—a cold and eerily dark evening that will stay with me for ever. My husband and I drove home along the main road from Oswestry to Nescliffe in the kind of rain that makes you shiver inside your clothes.

It had been good to spend the day with my brother and his grown-up family in Chirk, north Wales. It was a welcome chance to recharge our batteries after all the Christmas services we'd taken as a clergy couple. Evening crib services, midnight mass and early Christmas morning eucharists had all merged into one celebration as we exchanged hugs and presents with the family. Visiting Dave and Joan and their sons and three grandchildren had become a precious Boxing Day tradition and a God-given gift that we looked forward to during our busiest time in church. But now, it was 9pm on a truly filthy night and we would be so glad to get back to Cannock, Staffordshire, and the vicarage.

'Jesus!' It wasn't a blasphemy. The name came out of both of us in a simultaneous prayer as, out of nowhere, a tall, shambling figure in black appeared in our path on the road. It was a figure in a hood, walking away, filling the rain-lashed windscreen. There was no way Mark could avoid hitting him. It all happened in a split second: the looming figure, the thud of the impact, the windscreen on my side of the car shattering into a weird black spider's web before my eyes.

As the car stopped about 50 yards further on, Mark switched on the hazard lights. Then he jumped out and ran back to the scene. I hurriedly followed, aware of the cars zooming by on the dark road, and then of Mark flagging them down, calling out about finding someone with a mobile phone, still a fairly rare occurrence in those days.

The man was lying by the side of the road, a big, stationary hump. Already, miraculously, people were around him, trying to help, even though the road had seemed empty only moments before.

'Is he… dead?' I couldn't bear to look. It hadn't been our fault: he was in black clothes and had been walking in the middle of a main road, his back turned to the oncoming traffic. And yet, we might have killed him.

'No. He's been talking.' Mark put out his hand to me as more help arrived from passing cars. One tall man was an army paramedic; another said he was a fireman. Even in the midst of the trauma, those mere facts seemed so fortuitous that I gulped.

A young woman who had been first at the scene also had a mobile phone and had called the emergency services. The ambulance and police were on their way. Everything had simply been taken out of our hands, exactly how and when we needed it to be.

Through it all, the man we had knocked down lay in the gutter, covered with coats. He began to struggle, trying to sit up, and I saw that he was about 40 years old. His hood was down now, and his dark, curly hair was plastered to his head by the rain. He was confused and abusive, refusing to let anyone touch him, growling and lashing out, and it soon became clear that he was very drunk.

The rescue services arrived together, and soon there were flashing lights and policemen in fluorescent yellow coats, putting out cones and redirecting traffic around us. We told an officer what had happened and he came to look at our car before taking Mark into his panda car to make a statement. A message he sent via his radio quickly confirmed that the car we were driving hadn't been stolen. To think we might be suspected of being car thieves was sobering, to say the least, and for a split second it was as if we had been catapulted into a scary and unrecognizable world.

I was asked to wait in the car while Mark was interviewed and, as a matter of procedure, breathalysed. I didn't know what was happening to the man, but another ambulance arrived, and all I could do was to sit there behind the shattered windscreen, praying that he was going to be all right.

The eeriness of the night was intensified by my isolation and lingering sense of disbelief and horror. I kept reliving the moment the hooded figure had loomed into sight, and I wished I could be with Mark in the panda car, if only to hear what was being said. I knew Mark had had only one glass of wine, hours before, at lunchtime, so he was in no danger of being alcohol positive. But the time passed really slowly, and it was so surreal, being in the middle of flashing lights, seeing the police, glimpsing curious dark figures in the cars going by, watching heads turn in that almost hypnotic fascination that people seem to have when passing a road accident.

And yet, in the very strangeness of the situation, I felt around me a sense of presence almost impossible to put into words. The need to pray was very great and I sensed that I wasn't praying either alone or in vain. Someone or something was there—unseen, indescribable, but definitely present. And that someone or something was whispering that, impossible though it seemed, this ordeal would pass, for all concerned.

Eventually, the police officer came back with Mark, and another arrived on his heels. He told us that the man we had knocked down had refused to get into either of the two ambulances and had been taken home by the police. We were free to go, and there were no charges to answer.

With the broken windscreen letting the rain and darkness in, it was a long, cold journey back to Cannock. Mark was afraid to put the windscreen wipers on in case the whole thing collapsed on us, so we travelled very much in a spirit of trust, both unusually quiet and subdued. It was with a sigh of relief that we arrived home over an hour later. The rain had stopped, but the night was still heavy with gloom as we turned down the side of St Chad's church and up to the darkened vicarage.

In the study, the telephone was ringing, and Mark hurried to answer it while I went through putting on lights and drawing curtains. 'That was the police,' he said as he followed me into the living-room a few moments later. 'Apparently, the chap insisted they drop him outside his house, and then he walked up the path and went inside! I'll check again over the next few days to see if they hear any more. But they're saying at the police station that there must be somebody looking after him!'

'Us, too!' I shivered as I went to switch on the gas fire, reliving the surreal and frightening events of the evening, and the feeling, still hard to put into words, that we hadn't endured it on our own.

I thought of the helpers who had come out of an empty road with just the right skills and qualifications—and the sensation of company that I'd had while sitting praying in the car when our worst nightmares had seemed so close and real. It was exactly as if we, and the man who had stumbled drunkenly into the path of our moving car, had been under some form of protection, I pondered.

Then my eyes went to the coffee table, and the book, so far unread, that our grown-up daughter had given us, the day before, on Christmas Day: *Angels to Watch Over Me*.

1

ANGELS THEN AND NOW

This book is about angels—what and who they are, and the place they have in the scriptures. It is about the role of angels as they seem to be used by God as divine messengers and guardians in the lives of great Old Testament characters like Abraham and Jacob, Daniel and Elisha. It is about angels ministering to the early followers of Jesus, whose zeal for the gospel landed them in prison and in danger. Angels also appear as travelling companions, like the one who stood with Paul in the midst of a terrific storm at sea, and they carry home safely the servants of God who have finished their earthly life and long to see him face to face, like the first Christian martyr, Stephen.

In God's heavenly kingdom, the new Jerusalem, myriad angels are described as bowing down, day and night, ceaselessly worshipping him who is both holy and worthy (Revelation 4—5). The Bible says that angels also play an important part in carrying out God's final judgment, when, according to Jesus, the 'sheep' will be separated from the 'goats' (Matthew 25:31–33).

This book is also about people—not only the amazing multifarious cast of biblical characters, and a few taken from history and other works about angels, but ordinary men and women just like you and me, who are willing to testify to the existence of angels in their lives today. Some of their stories are similar to our Boxing Day road accident in that there was just a strong sense that 'someone' was taking care of them, while others report coming into contact with a being whose message, spoken or unspoken, changed their lives. This being may have looked like a human stranger, or have possessed the traditional heavenly attribute of wings, or have been identified only by extraordinary light, or gentle voices speaking or singing.

For others, an angel has been an unknown and unidentifiable comforting presence during an illness or after an operation. There are also some who believe that their most traumatic journeys have been shared by a special companion, sent specifically by God to make sure they reached their destination in safety.

Angels have also been glimpsed in worship, in sometimes quite unremarkable church buildings, inspiring a lifetime's wonder, or even in works of art. In a few cases, they have appeared to give a warning or to halt a catastrophe in a person's everyday life.

But what exactly are angels and what do we know about them?

First, the Bible says that, just like people, angels were made by God—they are part of his teeming creation—but they have greater power and knowledge than we do, and are certainly much more mobile. In the Bible, and in current personal experience, angels seem to appear within an instant, and the distance between heaven and earth is nothing to them.

The existence of angels is accepted by all three of the great Western religions, and they appear not only in the Bible but also in the Jewish Talmud and the Islamic Qur'an. The biblical tradition, further developed by the Church Fathers, is that angels are created, spiritual beings who assist God and make up the court of heaven (see Psalm 8:5; Job 1:6; 38:7) According to the book of Revelation, some of the angels got above themselves and wished to rule like God, and so there was a terrible war in heaven (Revelation 12:7). A fallen angel—Satan, also known as Lucifer—headed the rebellion, but was defeated, and roams the world to this day, intent upon tempting and possessing as his own the children of God.

Belief in angels was declared a dogma of the Church at the Council of Nicea in 325, but a later synod condemned the worship of angels—something also discouraged by scripture: 'Do not let anyone disqualify you, insisting on self-abasement and worship of angels, dwelling on visions, puffed up without cause by a human way of thinking' (Colossians 2:18).

According to the Qur'an, when human beings were created by God, the angels were required to bow down and worship them—an order that prompted Lucifer's rebellion. The prophet Muhammad also saw a beautiful vision of the angel Jabrail (Gabriel), who promised to guide him in his role as a newly chosen prophet.

The Greek philosopher Socrates believed in guardian angels, and many famous saints, including Francis of Assisi and Columba, also claimed to have seen them. Joan of Arc (1412–31) first heard the voice of an angel at the age of 13. She demanded an audience with Charles the Dauphin, heir to the French throne, telling him that she had a message from God. She led the Dauphin's army to victory, and at his coronation ceremony over 300 people were said to have seen an angel in their midst. In the 16th century, the Carmelite nun Teresa of Avila experienced visions and visitations from angels, which led to her famous writings, *The Way of Perfection*. Former American president Abraham Lincoln also frequently felt the presence of angels, as did General William Booth, the founder of the Salvation Army.

Angels appear in the writings of Shakespeare, Milton and Dante, as well as in the works of contemporary writers. It is, in fact, quite amazing to glance along a few shelves in a public library and note just how many books of all genres have the word 'angel' in their title.

There are nearly 300 references to angels in the Bible, 108 in the Old Testament and 165 in the much shorter New Testament. These spiritual beings are recorded as being used by God as messengers (the word for 'angel' actually means 'messenger' in both Greek and Hebrew). The angel Gabriel brings the news to Mary that she has been chosen to be the mother of our Lord, the shepherds are told by angels that Jesus has been born, and angels famously pass on the wonderful message of the resurrection.

According to the scriptures, angels are also employed by God to be the guardians of human beings: 'He will command his angels concerning you to guard you in all your ways,' says Psalm 91:11. And in Matthew 18:10, Jesus warns solemnly against harming little ones, because they have angels—angels who always behold the face of 'my father in heaven'.

The traditional Catholic belief in a personal guardian angel is a very comforting thought, and Mary, mother of Jesus, is believed to have been born with many such angels to guide and protect her. In spite of all his sufferings, the Old Testament prophet Job speaks of angels (Job 4:18), and God speaks to Job about them when he reminds him of his own human insignificance, in Job 38:4–7:

> *Where were you when I laid the foundation of the earth?*
> *Tell me, if you have understanding.*
> *Who determined its measurements—surely you know!*
> *Or who stretched the line upon it?*
> *On what were its bases sunk,*
> *or who laid its cornerstone*
> *when the morning stars sang together*
> *and all the heavenly beings shouted for joy?*

In the Psalms we read of angels comforting God's people and delivering them from all kinds of trouble and danger: 'The angel of the Lord encamps around those who fear him, and delivers them' (Psalm 34:7), while in the New Testament book of Acts, angels are recorded as ministering to the Lord's people at least six times.

Traditionally, angels have also been associated with travel: their emblems can be seen on the prows of old ships. It is interesting, therefore, that angels as travelling companions are featured in both the Old and New Testament, as well as the Apocrypha.

In the book of Genesis, the patriarch Abraham sends off the eldest of his servants on a mission to find a wife for his precious son Isaac, from among his relatives in the land from which God called him. Reassuringly, Abraham tells the servant, 'He will send his angel before you; you shall take a wife for my son from there' (Genesis 24:7). Moses also knew the companionship of angels. In his call to return to Egypt, the angel of the Lord appeared to him in a burning bush (Exodus 3:2), and angel travelled in front of

Israel's army at the crossing of the Red Sea (Exodus 14:19).

In the New Testament book of Colossians, Paul reminds us that all things were created by God, and all things existed through the supremacy of Jesus Christ: 'things visible and invisible, whether thrones or dominions or rulers or powers—all things have been created through him and for him' (Colossians 1:16).

It is said that the complex grouping of angels into ranks or 'hosts' is at least partly derived from the 'things invisible' in Colossians. The 13th-century theologian Thomas Aquinas described separate entities of angels, and placed them in three hierarchies, each having three categories. The highest are seraphim, cherubim and thrones; the middle rank are dominions, virtues and powers; and finally come principalities, archangels and angels.

Seraphim are described vividly in Isaiah 6, when the prophet had a vision of God in heaven. This is the only place in the Bible where seraphim or seraphs are mentioned specifically.

In the year that King Uzziah died, I saw the Lord sitting on a throne, high and lofty; and the hem of his robe filled the temple. Seraphs were in attendance above him; each had six wings: with two they covered their faces, and with two they covered their feet, and with two they flew. And one called to another and said: 'Holy, holy, holy is the Lord of hosts; the whole earth is full of his glory.'

The pivots on the thresholds shook at the voices of those who called, and the house filled with smoke. And I said: 'Woe is me! I am lost, for I am a man of unclean lips, and I live among a people of unclean lips; yet my eyes have seen the King, the Lord of hosts!'

Then one of the seraphs flew to me, holding a live coal that had been taken from the altar with a pair of tongs. The seraph touched my mouth with it and said: 'Now that this has touched your lips, your guilt has departed and your sin is blotted out.' Then I heard the voice of the Lord saying, 'Whom shall I send, and who will go for us?' And I said, 'Here am I; send me!'

ISAIAH 6:1–8

'Seraphim' means 'burning ones', from the Hebrew word *saraph*, to burn. These six-winged beings are positioned above God's throne and their whole purpose seems to be to praise his glory and holiness, though one of them has been chosen here by God to carry the burning coal to touch Isaiah's lips and so empower him to answer the call to be a prophet.

Cherubim, when referred to as 'cherubs', have become synonymous with those cute baby angels that we sometimes see on Christmas cards, but in the Bible cherubim are altogether much more muscular and scary! It was cherubim who were placed by God on the east side of the garden of Eden, together with a flaming sword, after Adam and Eve had been driven out of their paradise (Genesis 3:24). King David sang the praises of the Lord, thanking him for delivering him from the hands of his enemies, and describing how 'he rode on a cherub, and flew; he came swiftly upon the wings of the wind' (Psalm 18:10).

The prophet Ezekiel had many strange visions. While living in exile in Babylon, he prophesied the destruction of Jerusalem. Ezekiel saw 'the glory of the Lord' and, in the midst of lightning and fire and brilliant light, 'something like four living creatures' (Ezekiel 1:5). Each of the four creatures had two wings out-stretched, and another two wings covering the body. They moved speedily in any one of four directions, with the aid of wheels, and when the prophet saw the likeness that they worshipped, he fell face down.

Later in Ezekiel, these living creatures are called cherubim, and are described as being full of eyes and surrounded by wheels within wheels. In Ezekiel 9:3, the Lord has descended from his throne above the cherubim to the threshold of the temple, while in 10:1 he returns to take his seat above them. God's glory is to be withdrawn from Jerusalem, and the fluttering of the cherubim's many wings indicates this important event.

Images of cherubim are described as being fashioned in wood and gold elsewhere in the Bible. For example, these images stood as a guard to the precious ark of the covenant, which contained the tablets of stone inscribed with the Ten Commandments that God gave to Moses (Exodus 37:6–9), and eventually stood in the temple built by Solomon (1 Kings 6:23–28).

Other categories of angels do not seem so obviously present in the pages of scripture as do seraphim, cherubim, angels and archangels. According to medieval scholastic theologians, thrones and dominions are said to 'regulate angels' duties', while virtues work miracles on earth and powers protect us from demons. The role of principalities, archangels and angels is to be guardians and to minister to people.

The Bible does tell us that angels can be with us in a split second. They appear as 'men in white' (Acts 1:10), or as unexpected visitors bringing strange messages (Genesis 18:1–10); they hold swords (Numbers 22:23); they can open the doors of a jail (Acts 5:19) and shut the mouths of lions (Daniel 6:22). They also fly high in the air (Revelation 14:6) and stand on the sea (Revelation 10:5), and they fed Jesus in the wilderness (Matthew 4:11).

The angel Gabriel and the archangel Michael are the only angels actually named in the Bible. Gabriel's name, in Hebrew, means 'God's hero' or 'the mighty one'. He is seen very much as God's messenger, and the messages he brings are always good, if some-times startling, news! It was Gabriel who appeared to Daniel to explain the meaning of a vision (Daniel 9:21), to Zechariah to tell him his wife Elizabeth would have a son (Luke 1:19), and to Mary to bring her the amazing news that she would be the mother of Jesus (Luke 1:26).

Michael, the only designated archangel, is named in Jude 9, in Daniel 10:21, and also in Revelation 12:7: 'And war broke out in heaven; Michael and his angels fought against the dragon.' In the Old Testament, Michael seems to be used by God as a messenger of law and judgment especially in relation to God's people, Israel. His role throughout is one of battle against Satan, and his festival in the church calendar, 29 September, is significantly and deferentially known as 'St Michael and All Angels'.

Common to all angels are symbolic attributes of light, flight and heavenly beauty, and many are described as being clad in shining white robes, although some, like Daniel's 'man', are more strange and terrible to behold (Daniel 10:5–6).

Before the advent of science, angels were thought to be responsible for moving the stars and the elements, and for the phenomenon of gravity. During the Middle Ages, people believed in angels simply because they believed in God, and this was the time when many great works of art were created in which 'the bright birds of God', as Dante described them, were dramatically featured. Some angelic paintings show angels with all-seeing eyes in their wings or in the centre of their graceful hands, while others have peacock-feather plumage to symbolize the countless eyes of seraphim.

Over the centuries, certain other artistic traditions developed in the depiction of angels, many of them derived from scriptural descriptions. Gabriel carries a lily or a staff at the annunciation, or a trumpet at the last judgment. Michael wields a sword in battle against the forces of evil, and at the last judgment is depicted as carrying a pair of scales for balancing the souls of the dead. In Tintoretto's famous painting, *The Last Supper* (1594), there are several winged angels adding to the confusion of the scene as Jesus feeds his disciples on the night of his betrayal. Much later, the mystic William Blake (1757–1827) painted *Christ in the Sepulchre Guarded by Angels*, with two huge, hovering white figures, their wings joined in a kind of cradle over the still-sleeping Jesus.

In Victorian churchyards, like in our own present parish of Short Heath, Willenhall, there are several large stone angels, their grey wings outspread somewhat eerily as they point us back to a different age. Once magnificent, they are now neglected, guarding family graves that no longer have people to visit or tend them. They remind us that our great-grandparents had a particular attitude to death, and to mourning, giving these aspects of life a central place in their society.

Nowadays, plastic windmills, photographs and even soft toys have taken the place of graveside angels, but there is no less interest among the general public in these celestial beings. To enter the word 'angel' in an internet search engine is to discover some 364,000 sites in the UK and Ireland alone. Go into any gift shop, and you will find angels for everything, on pins and pictures, ornaments, clothing and statuettes. There are angels for aunties, angels for drivers, angels for just about every person and every occasion on the planet. Some people—obviously a lot of people—are laughing as they wing their way to the nearest bank!

But do angels really exist? Does God still send messengers and guardians to guide and protect us through our life on earth? Are there still heavenly presences hovering, ready to be instantly at hand when we need comfort or consolation? And when we travel, is there someone unseen always travelling with us, just waiting to be summoned by prayer, right up until the last journey we ever make— the journey from this earth and through the gates of heaven? In the words of the Victorian writer Samuel Butler, 'All reason is against it, and all healthy instinct is for it.'

The sceptic's view, of course, would be that to believe in such things is totally crazy. No one in their right mind would consider even for a moment that angels really exist, especially in our technological 21st century. But Paul says that our Christian faith is foolishness to the 'wise' of the world (1 Corinthians 1:18–24), and Jesus himself has told us that we should be prepared to believe in the pure and lovely way of children: 'Truly I tell you, whoever does not receive the kingdom of God as a little child will never enter it' (Mark 10:15). Meanwhile, there are thousands of people all over the world who believe that they have seen and sometimes talked with angels. A recent ITV poll states that one in three British people believes in angels, while a US Gallup poll suggests that more than 60 per cent of Americans also believe wholeheartedly in them.

Book after book has been written about angelic experiences, and some of the stories are truly wonderful and inspirational, especially when they point us directly back to God as the source of both the wonder and the inspiration. Many of the encounters described in these books are uncannily similar to one another. Complete strangers give information that changes people's lives. Silent combatants stand guard over a potential victim until a potential mugger or rapist gets 'cold feet'. Unforgettable doctors and nurses appear at bedsides at the most critical times, and are then not owned by hospital staff or authorities. There are also characters who appear out of nowhere when a journey is to be made, or give directions without being asked, and there are travelling-companion angels who, many people swear, come to collect us when our life on earth is done, taking us with them to a heaven where there will be worship, and also judgment.

As a priest serving in Black Country parishes of the West Midlands over the past 14 years, I also have been privileged to meet face to face many people who claim that their lives have been touched and transformed by angels. Although I myself cannot claim to have seen an angel, there was one night, many years ago, when I definitely heard them singing; and there have been certain times in my own ministry when I have known that God's angels were very near.

The truth is that it is all a mystery, but one thing I do know for certain is that *Assist Our Song* is a book that God definitely wanted me to write. Ever since I began to think about the project, there have been 'holy coincidences': angels in every magazine and newspaper, and in Sunday morning readings from the Bible, which have changed my preaching topic. I wasn't at all surprised that the contract arrived from the publishers on 29 September, when the Church celebrates Michael and All Angels.

The day I started writing the book, both of my daily devotional passages were about angels, and a funeral booked next day in church included a special song: 'Goodnight, my angel' by Billy Joel. In the evening, for a little light relief, I rang my friend. 'You just caught me,' she said, unknowingly. 'I've been busy all afternoon— cutting out angels for next week's Sunday school!'

Everlasting God, you have ordained and constituted the ministries of angels and mortals in a wonderful order: grant that as your holy angels always serve you in heaven, so, at your command, they may help and defend us on earth; through Jesus Christ you Son our Lord, who is alive and reigns with you, in the unity of the Holy Spirit, one God, now and for ever.

COLLECT FOR 29 SEPTEMBER, MICHAEL AND ALL ANGELS[1]

——— *2* ———

MESSENGERS IN THE
OLD TESTAMENT

The Lord appeared to Abraham by the oaks of Mamre, as he sat at
the entrance of his tent in the heat of the day. He looked up and
saw three men standing near him. When he saw them, he ran from
the tent entrance to meet them, and bowed down to the ground.
He said, 'My lord, if I find favour with you, do not pass by your
servant. Let a little water be brought, and wash your feet, and rest
yourselves under the tree. Let me bring a little bread, that you may
refresh yourselves, and after that you may pass on—since you
have come to your servant.' So they said, 'Do as you have said.'
And Abraham hastened into the tent to Sarah, and said, 'Make
ready quickly three measures of choice flour, knead it, and make
cakes.' Abraham ran to the herd, and took a calf, tender and good,
and gave it to the servant, who hastened to prepare it. Then he
took curds and milk and the calf that he had prepared, and set it
before them; and he stood by them under the tree while they ate.

They said to him, 'Where is your wife Sarah?' And he said,
'There, in the tent.' Then one said, 'I will surely return to you in
due season, and your wife Sarah shall have a son.'

GENESIS 18:1–10

Abraham (initially known as Abram) was the first patriarch, and was
born about 2160BC. The founder of the Hebrew nation, he is still
revered by Jews, Christians and Muslims, who all see him as the
great father-figure of faith. Abraham's universal appeal is his close
relationship with God. He was called God's friend (2 Chronicles

20:7; Isaiah 41:8). He built altars in order to invoke the name of the Lord, and the Lord spoke to him often, at great length and in hitherto unheard-of depth.

Abraham made mistakes, however. On two occasions, when it suited him, he lied and pretended that his wife Sarah was his sister (Genesis 12 and 20). But he always tried to be obedient to God, even to the point of being prepared to give his precious son Isaac as a sacrifice to the Lord (Genesis 22). His faith pleased God, and he became a figure of honour and example: 'And he believed the Lord; and the Lord reckoned it to him as righteousness' (Genesis 15:6).

Abraham is also frequently mentioned in the New Testament. His covenant relationship with the Lord is celebrated in the prophecy of Zechariah (Luke 1:72–74), and his example is upheld throughout Romans 4, where he is declared righteous by faith (v. 3) and 'the father of all of us' (v. 16). In the letter of James, Abraham's unquestioning willingness to offer Isaac as a sacrifice is commended (James 2:21), while in the panoramic history of faith set down in the letter to the Hebrews, Abraham's faith is an inspiring example of how a life, and a people, can be changed by 'the assurance of things hoped for, the conviction of things not seen' (Hebrews 11:1).

Abram originally came from Ur of the Chaldeans, a Sumerian city in the Euphrates valley near the head of the Persian Gulf. With his father Terah, his wife Sarai (later Sarah) and his nephew Lot, he moved up the river to Haran. The family settled there, and it was the place where Terah died. In Genesis 12, we read that the Lord appeared to Abram at Haran and told him to leave for 'the land that I will show you' (v. 1). The Lord promised that he would make of Abram 'a great nation' and would bless him (v. 2). Abram was then 75 years old, but he obeyed without question the call to move. With Sarai and Lot, he travelled to Canaan and reached Shechem. The Lord then appeared to him again, saying, 'To your offspring I will give this land' (v. 7). So he built an altar to the Lord at Shechem, and another altar near to Bethel, a little north of Jerusalem, showing that his impulse was always to give thanks.

The promise was repeated during Abram's lifetime, even though he had, as yet, no descendants. God continued to lead him where he wanted him to go. When Abram was 99, and Sarai 90, the Lord appeared to him once again and said that henceforth his name would be Abraham, 'for I have made you the ancestor of a multitude of nations' (Genesis 17:5). Sarai's name was changed to Sarah ('princess'). She would be blessed by God and would give Abraham a son, whom he would call Isaac. As a sign of the covenant made that day, Abraham was instructed to circumcise himself and all male members of his household, and thereafter every male infant when eight days old.

The appearance of the three men to Abraham by the oaks of Mamre in Genesis 18 is the first biblical indication that God's angels might appear in human form and interact with human beings. It is an atmospheric account of something that happened one shimmering noontide, while the old man sat sheltering in the entrance to his tent.

The presence of strangers at that moment would have seemed odd, to say the least. It was customary and sensible to stay out of the sun at the hottest part of the day, and tent dwellers were grateful for the shade of their awnings. Despite the incongruity of the visit and the heat of the day, Abraham rose and ran to greet his unexpected guests. He honoured them with impeccable eastern hospitality: bowing to the ground, and offering them the refreshment of foot-washing, rest and food.

There are echoes here of the well-known exhortation in the New Testament letter to the Hebrews: 'Do not neglect to show hospitality to strangers, for by doing that some have entertained angels without knowing it' (Hebrews 13:2). The writer of Hebrews is thought to be referring specifically to Abraham's perfect reception of his heavenly visitors, the leader of whom is clearly identified as the Lord (Genesis 18:1).

These same visitors were immortalized by the Russian painter Andrei Rublev. Around 1410, he created the now-famous icon that depicts the Holy Trinity visiting Abraham that day. There is a gentle purposefulness about the three figures shown sitting round

Abraham's table, on which is set a dish of food. They are reclining, their beautiful robes draped gracefully around them, their golden wings at rest. In some versions of Rublev's work, Sarah is shown, peeping curiously in on the scene.

It is impossible to know for certain the identity of these strange and unexpected guests, but by the oaks of Mamre Sarah was called upon to make cakes of bread, and the servant was ordered to prepare the finest calf. Together with curds and milk, Abraham set out this feast and then stood respectfully by, presumably to make sure everyone was satisfied.

'Where is your wife Sarah?' The meal over, the conversation now focused on the real reason for the visitation, which was the foretelling of the future. The time was fixed when Sarah would have the son already promised by God. We read that Sarah, listening at the entrance to the tent, laughed to herself at such an idea (Genesis 18:12). She was, after all, 90 years old, well past child-bearing age. Abraham had also laughed—had, in fact, laughed so much that he fell over—when God first gave him the news: 'Then Abraham fell on his face and laughed, and said to himself, "Can a child be born to a man who is a hundred years old? Can Sarah, who is ninety years old, bear a child?"' (Genesis 17:17). Yet, because nothing is too wonderful for the Lord (Genesis 18:14), the message that the three supernatural visitors brought to Mamre that day came miraculously true. In the fullness of time, along came Isaac, whose name, not so coincidentally, means 'laughter'!

In Genesis 28, we find the story of a dream of angels as experienced by Abraham's grandson Jacob (the son of Isaac), who lived around 2006BC. The dream took place when Jacob, an impetuous, rather greedy young man, was fleeing from the righteous anger of his twin brother Esau, whom he had cheated out of his birthright.

The story really begins with the birth of these two brothers, who struggled together within their mother Rebekah's womb: 'And the Lord said to her, "Two nations are in your womb, and two peoples born of you shall be divided; one shall be stronger than the other, the elder shall serve the younger' (Genesis 25:23). Jacob, the younger, came into the world gripping his brother Esau's heel, and the twins effectively divided their parents, because as they grew up 'Isaac loved Esau, because he was fond of game; but Rebekah loved Jacob' (v. 28).

It was Esau's love of game that led to his being robbed of his birthright. One day, when Jacob was cooking a meal of stew, Esau came in, famished, from hunting. He asked his brother for some of the stew, and Jacob craftily suggested that Esau pay for it with his birthright. At that time, and in that culture, a birthright could be sold or given away, but such an action was not considered lightly because the birthright was a special honour, given to the firstborn son. It included a double portion of the family inheritance along with the honour of one day being head of the family. Feeling that he was about to die from hunger, Esau agreed to the bargain and swore an oath to Jacob that the birthright now belonged to him. 'Thus,' Genesis tells us, 'Esau despised his birthright' (v. 34).

But it was only after Jacob, led on by his doting mother, deceived again—this time tricking his father Isaac into giving him his blessing—that Esau realized just how thoroughly he had been duped. The father's blessing was needed in order to make the brothers' contract binding. 'Is he not rightly named Jacob?' Esau cried. 'For he has supplanted me these two times. He took away my birthright; and look, now he has taken away my blessing!' (Genesis 27:36). Esau, understandably, now hated Jacob, and swore to kill him. Rebekah, ever protective of her favourite son, arranged for Jacob to go to Haran, to her brother Laban, and Isaac charged him to take a wife from among Laban's daughters.

Jacob set off on his journey. Darkness fell, and in the wilderness, in the place where his grandfather Abraham had built one of his many altars to the Lord, he lay down with a stone for his pillow. He fell into an exhausted sleep, and almost immediately began to dream. 'And he dreamed that there was a ladder set up on the earth, the top of it reaching to heaven; and the angels of God were ascending and descending on it' (Genesis 28:12).

The image is one of grace and movement, and the significance of the fact that the angels were ascending *and* descending is not lost. (If some were ascending, they must have been already here, on the earth.) The message of those angels was given by the Lord himself, who stood beside Jacob in his dream. In an echo of the words of the covenant he had made with Abraham, God reiterated his promise to give the land on which Jacob lay to him and his descendants: 'Know that I am with you and will keep you wherever you go, and will bring you back to this land; for I will not leave you until I have done what I have promised you' (v. 15).

This dream was a sign that, despite Jacob's shady past, the God of his father Isaac and grandfather Abraham wanted to be his God, too. Jacob woke and was afraid, filled with awe by the place, which he recognized as the house of God and the gate of heaven. But he was also heartened and excited by the message that had been brought to him so dramatically.

He set up the stone on which he had lain, and poured oil on it, making a ceremony of naming the place 'Bethel' ('house of God'). 'Then Jacob made a vow, saying, "If God will be with me, and will keep me in this way that I go, and will give me bread to eat and clothing to wear, so that I come again to my father's house in peace, then the Lord shall be my God, and this stone, which I have set up for a pillar, shall be God's house; and of all that you give me I will surely give one-tenth to you"' (vv. 20–22).

Already, Jacob was beginning to be a changed man—a process for which the Lord had definitely used his holy angels. They would be used several more times before Jacob's life on earth was ended, and he would thank God for them.

Some 300 years later, the 80-year-old patriarch Moses was visited by the angel of the Lord in a burning bush, which, although on fire, was not consumed. Moses, like Jacob, had been chosen by God for a specific task. It seemed typically impossible. Moses was to go to Pharaoh, who held the descendants of Jacob in bondage in Egypt, and demand of him, 'Let my people go!'

Although brought up as a wealthy and powerful Egyptian, Moses was a Hebrew with a heart for the abused and downtrodden Hebrew people. He had, in fact, killed an Egyptian for beating one of his kinsmen, and been forced to flee for his life to the desert, where he became a lowly shepherd.

In Exodus 3, the angel of the Lord is synonymous with the Lord himself, and it was with the Lord that Moses rightly argued, afraid that he would not be equal to the task: 'But Moses said to God, "Who am I that I should go to Pharaoh, and bring the Israelites out of Egypt?"' (v. 11). God's answer was another covenant: a solemn promise of future worship on the holy mountain, on the slopes of which Moses was now standing. This worship would doubtless include angels in its midst.

There are many other references in the Old Testament to angels appearing as messengers. In some cases, notably in Genesis 18, at the oaks of Mamre, it is thought by some theologians that Jesus himself appeared in angelic form, prior to his incarnation, and was called 'the Lord' or the 'angel of the Lord'. Visible appearances of Jesus in other forms prior to his incarnation are known as 'theophanies'.

The 'angel of the Lord' has also been variously identified as the archangels Michael or Gabriel, while in the writings of Daniel he is described as 'a man'—but a man such as even the visionary Daniel had never seen before: 'His body was like beryl, his face like lightning, his eyes like flaming torches, his arms and legs like the gleam of burnished bronze, and the sound of his words like the roar of a multitude' (Daniel 10:6).

The book of Daniel was written at a time when the Jewish people were in the throes of a severe crisis, living in exile in Babylon, in or around the sixth century BC. The worship of God was forbidden, the scriptures were publicly burnt, and possession of a copy of the Torah, the law of Moses, had been made punishable by death. Sabbath observance was also abolished, and the circumcision of infants (the covenant sign that God had given to Abraham) was declared illegal.

Daniel's angel—and the angel's message—had to be strong, and the 'man' described how he had had to be strengthened against evil powers on his mission by the archangel Michael, and how the fight between good and evil was real and unending: 'He said, "Do not fear, greatly beloved, you are safe. Be strong and courageous!" When he spoke to me, I was strengthened and said, "Let my lord speak, for you have strengthened me"' (Daniel 10:19). Daniel was encouraged to be daring by several other encounters with angels, one of whom was a guardian who shut the mouths of lions (6:22), while another, who had 'the appearance of a god', walked with his three friends Shadrach, Meshach and Abednego in the midst of a fiery blaze (Daniel 3:25).

The angels who brought messages to God's people in the pages of the Old Testament were fulfilling a vital role in the history of those people. They seemed to appear in times of crisis, like those suffered by the children of Israel in Egypt and Babylon. God wanted to save his people, to remind them of the words in Isaiah 41:10: 'Do not fear, for I am with you, do not be afraid, for I am your God; I will strengthen you, I will help you, I will uphold you with my victorious right hand.' These angels brought messages about nations, about laws, about battles and territory, prophecy and judgment, and about how the people of Israel should live, because God their Father was, and still is, intensely concerned about all these things.

But God's angels also brought news of relatively insignificant, personal events—like the birth of a totally unexpected child. Sarah was told by angels, one of whom might have been Jesus himself, that she was to be the mother of Isaac. And in Judges 13:3, Manoah received a shock when an angel of the Lord appeared to his wife and told her, 'Although you are barren, having borne no children, you shall conceive and bear a son' (v. 3). Manoah and his wife became the parents of a very great Israelite called Samson.

The very fact that God uses his special envoys to deliver what some might consider mundane messages proves how important such missions are to him, for they clear a flight path, and prepare the way for Jesus.

—— *3* ——

MESSENGERS IN THE NEW TESTAMENT

In the sixth month the angel Gabriel was sent by God to a town in Galilee called Nazareth, to a virgin engaged to a man whose name was Joseph, of the house of David. The virgin's name was Mary. And he came to her and said, 'Greetings, favoured one! The Lord is with you.' But she was much perplexed by his words and pondered what sort of greeting this might be. The angel said to her, 'Do not be afraid, Mary, for you have found favour with God. And now, you will conceive in your womb and bear a son, and you will name him Jesus. He will be great, and will be called the Son of the Most High, and the Lord God will give to him the throne of his ancestor David. He will reign over the house of Jacob for ever, and of his kingdom there will be no end.' Mary said to the angel, 'How can this be, since I am a virgin?' The angel said to her, 'The Holy Spirit will come upon you, and the power of the Most High will overshadow you; therefore the child to be born will be holy; he will be called Son of God. And now, your relative Elizabeth in her old age has also conceived a son; and this is the sixth month for her who was said to be barren. For nothing will be impossible with God.' Then Mary said, 'Here am I, the servant of the Lord; let it be with me according to your word.' Then the angel departed from her.

LUKE 1:26–38

This is possibly the most famous encounter of all time with a messenger angel. What a message—and what an angel! As God's special envoy, Gabriel is accorded a place in the Bible second only to the archangel Michael. He appears twice in the book of Daniel (8:16–26; 9:21–27) to interpret visions, and he also appears at the beginning of Luke's Gospel to announce another miraculous birth. In Luke 1, we read how the priest Zechariah was told by an angel that his elderly wife Elizabeth would conceive a son. The angel identified himself: 'I am Gabriel. I stand in the presence of God, and I have been sent to speak to you and to bring you this good news' (v. 19). Zechariah, perhaps naturally, questioned the validity of the message. Like Abraham and Sarah, he and Elizabeth were both getting on in years, and he asked how they could possibly become parents. As a punishment for this moment of doubt, the old man was told that he would be mute, unable to speak, until the day the angel's words came true (v. 20).

Gabriel's words did come true and Elizabeth eventually gave birth to John. Zechariah's mouth was opened and his tongue freed at last. The Bible tells us that when he began to speak, he began simultaneously to praise God. 'What then will this child become?' was the question being asked among Zechariah and Elizabeth's neighbours (v. 66). And the child, of course, became John the Baptist, the 'voice in the wilderness' who heralded the coming of Jesus, child of Mary, Son of God.

We are not told what time of day it was when Gabriel appeared to Mary, but in medieval paintings of the annunciation, the young peasant girl is portrayed as being busy about her household tasks. The strangeness of the angel's greeting seems to have startled her as much as his sudden appearance: 'Greetings, favoured one! The Lord is with you' (v. 28). As she pondered this, Gabriel reassured Mary that there was no need to be afraid, because she had found favour with Almighty God. The world-changing power of the message, and the power of the one who sent it, rang in his words as he gave her the amazing news that she was to be the mother of the Son of the Most High: 'He will reign over the house of Jacob for ever, and of his kingdom there will be no end' (v. 33).

With the benefit of hindsight, we can rejoice over the accuracy of that prophecy as we live in the knowledge of all that God has done for us through the death and resurrection of Jesus Christ. But Mary's question was of the moment, a simple and practical one that seems to sum up her whole personality. She wanted to know how she could possibly be the mother of God's son when she was a virgin.

Her engagement to Joseph, the respectable carpenter, was not mentioned either by her or by Gabriel, but betrothal in those days was as binding as marriage, and the penalty for being unfaithful was death by stoning. Mary could have been shackled in disgrace outside her father's house, and Joseph, the injured party, would have had the right to throw the first stone.

As Mary listened to Gabriel's explanation—that she would conceive by the power of the Holy Spirit, that the power of the Most High would overshadow her—she must have sensed that, somehow, Joseph's part in this astonishing drama had already been considered. She was able to remain calm as the mighty angel told her that the child she would bear would be holy—called the 'Son of God' (v. 35).

Further encouragement came in Gabriel's next words, in their way almost as amazing as the ones he had just imparted. Her elderly relative Elizabeth, known to bear the stigma of barrenness, had also conceived a son, and was in the sixth month of her pregnancy.

Mary's response to the angel is as famous as the encounter itself. It echoes through the ages, along with the Magnificat, the song she sang when she later visited Elizabeth and Elizabeth's child leapt with joy in her womb at the sight of 'the mother of my Lord' (v. 43). 'Here am I, the servant of the Lord,' Mary said. Devoted and dedicated, Mary gave her own message to Gabriel, a message of humility but also great courage as she looked ahead to probable disgrace and alienation: 'Let it be with me according to your word' (v. 38).

We are not told if it was Gabriel who also visited Joseph, but in Matthew 1:20–21 Mary's betrothed was also brought a message by an angel of the Lord. The angel said that Joseph should not be afraid to take Mary as his wife, for the baby conceived in her was from the Holy Spirit: 'She will bear a son, and you are to name him Jesus, for he will save his people from their sins.'

In the second chapter of Luke's Gospel, we read the familiar Christmas story of shepherds living in the fields, keeping watch over their flocks by night. The flocks reserved for temple sacrifice were kept in the fields near Bethlehem throughout the year, and in all kinds of weather. The shepherds' job would be to care for the sheep as well as to guard them against predatory animals and thieves. 'Then an angel of the Lord stood before them, and the glory of the Lord shone around them, and they were terrified. But the angel said to them, "Do not be afraid; for see—I am bringing you good news of great joy for all the people: to you is born this day in the city of David a Saviour, who is the Messiah, the Lord"' (Luke 2:9–11).

The shepherds were told that the child would be found wrapped in bands of cloth and lying in a manger. At the mention of this very significant sign of humility and vulnerability, the sky was suddenly —in the words of the carol, 'Ding dong, merrily on high'—'riven with angels singing'. There appeared 'a multitude of the heavenly host, praising God and saying, "Glory to God in the highest heaven, and on earth peace among those whom he favours!"' (v. 14).

After the angels left them, the shepherds went quickly to Bethlehem, to investigate for themselves the amazing event that God had told them about. The fact that simple shepherds had been chosen to receive this message would have been remarkable. The Messiah had been eagerly awaited for many centuries. Astrologers studied the stars, and kings held their breath. Shepherds were beyond the pale—simple, uneducated people who lived with livestock and were never able to get to the temple to worship because of the nature of their work.

The messenger angels changed their lives, opening their eyes to what God was capable of doing and giving. In the Eastern Orthodox tradition, Jesus is said to have been born in a hillside cave, a setting very similar to the tomb where he was laid after his crucifixion. But the shepherds did not know that the baby they found in the manger was to grow up to die a hideous death. That sad and shadowy knowledge existed only in the mind of God, and in the gift of myrrh, brought as a gift for a king (Matthew 2:11), and applied to his body after his death (John 19:39–40).

Yet there was something of the glory of the resurrection in the shepherds' homage to the Christ-child in their dirty clothes, carrying their sticks and their baby lambs—as if all the world was holding its breath, and has been, every Christmas Eve ever since, recognizing this most holy of holy nights when angels sang and shepherds were summoned to worship.

The news of the resurrection, over three decades later, was again brought by an angel, according to Matthew's Gospel. After the crucifixion and burial of Jesus in the guarded tomb of Joseph of Arimathea, Mary Magdalene and the other Mary went to see the tomb (Matthew 28:1). 'And suddenly there was a great earthquake; for an angel of the Lord, descending from heaven, came and rolled back the stone and sat on it. His appearance was like lightning, and his clothing white as snow. For fear of him the guards shook and became like dead men' (vv. 2–4). The angel addressed the women, telling them not to be afraid—the same words that had been spoken to Mary, Joseph and the shepherds at the start of Jesus' earthly life.

'I know that you are looking for Jesus who was crucified,' the angel continued. 'He is not here; for he has been raised, as he said. Come, see the place where he lay. Then go quickly and tell his disciples, "He has been raised from the dead, and indeed he is going ahead of you to Galilee; there you will see him." This is my message for you' (vv. 5–7).

This angel was not only dressed in white, but shone like a flash of brilliant lightning, and his image persists as a symbol of resurrection even in today's cinematic art. The beautiful, under-stated ending of Mel Gibson's 2004 film *The Passion of the Christ* is all aglow with the deep and mysterious aura of the angel who rolled away the stone.

This glory is enhanced rather than diminished by the fact that in Mark's account, there is 'a young man, dressed in a white robe', sitting in the tomb where Jesus had lain (16:5). Luke, meanwhile, describes the sudden appearance of 'two men in dazzling clothes' (24:4). In John's Gospel, the tomb is empty, but it is Jesus himself who appears to Mary Magdalene, making her, in that glorious encounter, the first witness to his resurrection.

There are many other places in the New Testament where message-bearing angels appear. In the book of Acts, we read the story of a Roman centurion called Cornelius:

He was a devout man who feared God with all his household; he gave alms generously to the people and prayed constantly to God. One afternoon at about three o'clock he had a vision in which he clearly saw an angel of God coming in and saying to him, 'Cornelius.' He stared at him in terror and said, 'What is it, Lord?' He answered, 'Your prayers and your alms have ascended as a memorial before God. Now send men to Joppa for a certain Simon who is called Peter; he is lodging with Simon, a tanner, whose house is by the seaside.' When the angel who spoke to him had left, he called two of his slaves and a devout soldier from the ranks of those who served him, and after telling them everything, he sent them to Joppa.

ACTS 10:2–8

This angel, like the angel of the resurrection, is described as wearing 'dazzling clothes' (10:30). His intervention was vital, because Cornelius was a Gentile, and Peter had just had a vision which clearly showed him that the gospel of Jesus Christ was not only for the Jews but for the whole wide world. Peter had seen a large sheet coming down from heaven, containing all kinds of animals, reptiles and birds that were ritually unclean in Jewish law, and therefore not fit to eat. A voice invited him to kill something and eat it, but Peter refused because, as a strict Hebrew, he had 'never eaten anything that is profane or unclean' (v. 14). The voice, coming a second time, reprimanded Peter: 'What God has made clean, you must not call profane' (v. 16).

It was while Peter was puzzling about this vision that the message came from Cornelius, saying that he had been directed by an angel to send for Peter and hear what he had to say. Although it was not lawful for a Jew to enter a Gentile house, Peter gladly visited Cornelius and spoke to an assembly of his family and friends. He told them all about Jesus, totally convinced that God had used an angel and a vision to ensure that the good news was not for one nation alone but for the salvation of the whole world.

In Acts 8, we read the encouraging story of the apostle Philip and his encounter with another Gentile, an Ethiopian eunuch. The story begins with an angel of the Lord directing Philip, 'Get up and go towards the south to the road that goes down from Jerusalem to Gaza' (v. 26). This road ran through the wilderness, and it was there that he passed the eunuch, a court official of the queen of the Ethiopians. The eunuch had come to Jerusalem to worship, and was returning home in his chariot, reading from the prophet Isaiah. Through the power of the Holy Spirit, Philip was able to guide the man in his reading, and, answering his questions, tell him the good news about Jesus.

The Ethiopian was so bowled over by what he heard that he requested baptism there and then, in the next available pool of water. He had been seeking truth and meaning to his life, and suddenly here it was. There was no need, or time, for delay. 'When they came up out of the water, the Spirit of the Lord snatched Philip away; the eunuch saw him no more, and went on his way rejoicing' (v. 39). The Ethiopian's euphoria was also carried by Philip, who, finding himself in the Philistine city of Azotus, continued to proclaim the good news to everyone he met.

The ascension of Jesus was attended by two angels in white robes, who again brought a profoundly important message, perhaps the most important message that has ever been heard. Jesus had just told his disciples that they would be his witnesses in all the world, working and living in the power of the Holy Spirit, which would come down on them from God. It was as Jesus was actually ascending into heaven in a cloud that 'two men in white robes' suddenly appeared. 'They said, "Men of Galilee, why do you stand looking up towards heaven? This Jesus, who has been taken up from you into heaven, will come in the same way as you saw him go into heaven"' (Acts 1:11).

Like other angelic messengers in the New Testament, these visitors are heralds of Jesus. Such angels appear at the focal points of his conception and birth, and at his resurrection. They give us the firm assurance that one day, when we least expect it, Jesus will return. They also help to establish the ministry he left for his followers to continue, a ministry that brings good news not to one nation but to the whole of the world. There is life-changing joy as well as continuity in the story these angels unfold. No wonder, over passing centuries, they have been the inspiration for so many hymns and Christmas carols!

4

MESSENGERS: PERSONAL EXPERIENCES

My stepson, Dr Edmund Hathorne, has excelled in his postgraduate scientific studies, and we are very proud of him, but there was a time, when he was coming up to his GCSE exams, when he had little motivation. 'I was travelling to school on several buses each day,' he reminds me. 'I was bored with lessons, unsociable at home and interested only in shutting myself in my room listening to reggae music!'

To express his teenage angst, Ed not only sported a weird hairstyle (shaved underneath and what I called 'floppy blond page-boy' on top). He also wore a distinctive woolly hat that did nothing to enhance the uniform of the prestigious Birmingham grammar school where he was a reluctant fifth-year pupil.

'One evening, I was on the last of my daily buses, the only passenger on the top deck,' he recounts. 'All of a sudden somebody banged really hard on the side of the bus as it slowed down to go round a corner in between stops. The driver let this guy get on and he came straight upstairs—a tall, thin West Indian guy in a huge Rastafarian hat, striped from top to bottom. Underneath, I could tell he had all these massive dreadlocks, and I couldn't help but stare! He sat on the seat across the aisle from me and said, "Hey, man! I like your hat!" I told him I liked his too, and we got talking. He asked me about school, and I told him I was supposed to be revising for some seriously uncool exams.'

Ed expected the stranger to sympathize. There was nothing

'uncool' about him! But to his surprise, the Rastafarian, looking deadly serious, said, 'Well, man, I never had no time for education and all that stuff. Now, I wish I had. I'm telling you, you're going to make a difference to this world—make it a better place. But to do it, you'll need those qualifications. You can't blow it, man—you've got to do the best you can!'

Ed continues, 'Then he stood up, went down the stairs and got off the bus as it slowed round another corner. He hadn't got on at a bus stop or waited to get off at one. He just disappeared.

'I know it sounds crazy,' my stepson finishes, 'but from then on, my attitude changed. I knew I had to work—that the message I'd been given was really important, and also that I wouldn't have accepted it from anybody else. If God was going to send me an angel at that particular part of my life, it needed to be a Rastafarian one! I never saw the man again, even though I travelled that same route at the same time nearly every day for over another year, and I kept on looking for him.'

Ed's messenger angel was real and tangible enough, even for a scientist, and he still believes in him and his message as he continues to work and to study in order to make the world a better place.

An experience similar to Ed's is described in detail in Hope Price's book, *Angels*, subtitled 'True stories of how they touch our lives'. She tells how a man called Kenneth Durbridge sat on a wall, waiting for the bus to take him to work. He had caught a bus there most days for 25 years. On this occasion, a stranger was sitting on the wall, and he stood up and approached Kenneth and asked him, 'What is the most important thing in your life?'

Taken aback, Kenneth replied that the most important thing in his life was his Christian faith. The man turned and looked him full in the face. 'That is a very good answer.' He then went on to explain how much God loved Kenneth and how important it is to live by the teachings of Jesus Christ.

Kenneth continues, 'Just then, the bus arrived, but the man stayed sitting on the wall. I got on the bus and turned to wave to him, but the wall was empty.'

Kenneth is convinced that this stranger was an angel with a very significant message from God. 'At that time I was trying to relate Darwin's theory of evolution to the teachings of the Bible, and I had come to the end of my tether. At this point I decided to pray that God should reveal the truth to me, if it was his will.'[2]

There are many other recorded stories of remarkable strangers who have brought unexpected or startling messages, or who have simply known things about someone without ever having been told.

Alice, a member of the Willenhall Christian Fellowship, where I sometimes preach, has worked with her husband Bill as a mission partner in Guyana and will happily describe canoeing up rainforest rivers to share worship in the remotest areas imaginable. The first time the couple felt God calling them to Guyana, however, Alice was understandably nervous.

'Everything seemed to be going wrong with our preparations,' she told me over coffee one day after church. 'And to cap it all, the week before we were due to leave, there was a terrible storm and several tiles blew off our roof. I went to the builders' yard to look for some new ones, and the first person I saw was a small, wiry black man with a shock of white hair. I asked him about the tiles, and he walked round with me to where they were.

'As we walked, he suddenly started talking as if he knew all about where Bill and I were going. He told me, "You'll tell people about Jesus Christ. Some will listen, but others won't." By the time I got the tiles and went to pay for them, he was gone, and when I asked about him, no one seemed to know who I was talking about. I'm convinced he was an angel, sent by God to encourage me for the future.'

While I was listening to Alice's story, a lady called June came up with one of her own. 'My friend Ann had been going out with a man called Brian for about ten years, but he seemed frightened of commitment,' she said as she joined us at our table. 'Whenever the subject of marriage came up, he made excuses: his job wasn't secure, he didn't have enough money, and so on. One day, the couple went into Birmingham and Ann left him outside St Martin's church while she went shopping. He was just standing there, minding his own business, when a man, a complete stranger, came up to him and said, "It's about time you got married!"

'Brian was absolutely dumbfounded. But before he could answer, the man had gone. Seconds later, he looked across to the main road, and there he was, sitting looking through the upstairs window of a passing bus. He waved to Brian and gave him a "thumbs up" sign, as if telling him it was OK to follow his advice. When Ann came back to the church, Brian promptly proposed, and she accepted. They're both certain that the stranger was an angel, and also that God has got a brilliant sense of humour!'

How can we explain such encounters? Some might say that the 'messengers' are just ordinary human beings coincidentally in the right place at the right time, or that such is our need for direction and guidance at certain times in our lives that we somehow engineer a meeting with someone who will say the words we need to hear.

Adele, another friend from church, has a very different outlook, and a vivid experience to share. 'One night, before I became a Christian, I met an angel face to face,' she says. 'I woke up, and there was a young man sitting on the side of my bed. He had wavy fair hair, old-fashioned-looking and rather long. He was just looking at me, as if he knew something I didn't.

'I turned to my husband and said, "There's a man on the bed!"

'He was half asleep, and muttered, "Don't be ridiculous!"

'I looked back, expecting the angel to have gone, but he was still there. He carried on looking at me, so deeply and sympathetically, and I closed my eyes and went to sleep.

'Soon after, my mother died, and I was plunged into a period of grief. I knew then that the angel had come to prepare me, even though his message was a silent one. It was not long afterwards that I accepted Jesus into my life.'

In Adele's experience, then, angels do not have to speak in order to deliver their messages. Indeed, such is the power and mystery of God the Holy Spirit that it is not always necessary for angels to be seen by human eyes for them to pass on what God wants us to know or do.

The last personal experience in this section comes from Daisy Munn, one of the founder members of St Aiden's Anglican church in Leamore, Walsall, a church on a housing estate where there are many social problems. The church has recently celebrated 40 years of Christian outreach there.

Daisy writes, 'At the time, my twin sons were in primary school, and it was my practice to pick them up as they came out, to walk them home safely. On one occasion, I got off the bus at the stop near the school but found myself walking in the opposite direction, towards my mother's house.

'I thought to myself, "Why on earth am I going this way, when I know that the school is the other way?" But I felt compelled, in a really strange way, to continue on to my mum's house, almost as if someone was whispering it into my ears. I knew that my friend would take my boys home with her son, and I needn't worry about them.

'When I got to my mother's, I found her in great distress. She was on the floor, with the German Shepherd dog that my brother had rescued from the local animal sanctuary standing over her. It wouldn't let her get up, and was growling, ready to attack her.

'I chased the dog off with the handy broom, and helped Mum to her feet. Over a cup of tea, she told me that she had lain there for half an hour, just praying that I would come to visit her!

'I believe the Lord had heard her prayer, and took me over, bodily, so that I was able to rescue her. (The dog was returned to the sanctuary, and they explained that it had been ill-treated by its previous owner.)'

Most Christians can recall occasions when such 'coincidences' have happened, and they have found themselves walking to a certain address, or picking up the telephone to ring someone who just 'happened' to be in need of some help and had been praying that God will somehow get a message through to the exact person who can supply it. As I have researched this book, I have become more and more convinced that many seeming coincidences are really angels at work, passing on vital news through the power of the Holy Spirit.

The poet John Milton wrote that God comes to visit us, and is delighted to send his 'winged messengers on errands of supernal grace'. In the Black Country, where angel sightings are still being reported, we put it more simply and bluntly: 'If the Lord don't come—he sends!'

✣

Make yourself familiar with the angels, and behold them frequently in spirit, for without being seen, they are present with you.
ST FRANCIS DE SALES (1567–1622)

Good angels, messengers of God,
protect us from all that would plague our bodies,
protect us from all that would plague our souls.
ST COLUMBA (521–597)

Dear Lord, we praise and bless you for the ministry of your messenger angels, both in the holy scriptures and in our daily lives. Please help us to keep open the ears of our hearts and minds, so that we may be willing receivers of your special ambassadors and the words they bring us from your heavenly throne. Amen.

---- *5* ----

GUARDIANS IN THE
OLD TESTAMENT

When an attendant of the man of God rose early in the morning
and went out, an army with horses and chariots was all around the
city. His servant said, 'Alas, master! What shall we do?' He replied,
'Do not be afraid, for there are more with us than there are with
them.' Then Elisha prayed: 'O Lord, please open his eyes that he
may see.' So the Lord opened the eyes of the servant, and he saw;
the mountain was full of horses and chariots of fire all around
Elisha. When the Arameans came down against him, Elisha
prayed to the Lord, and said, 'Strike this people, please, with
blindness.' So he struck them with blindness as Elisha had asked.
Elisha said to them, 'This is not the way, and this is not the city;
follow me, and I will bring you to the man whom you seek.' And
he led them to Samaria.

As soon as they entered Samaria, Elisha said, 'O Lord, open the
eyes of these men so that they may see.' The Lord opened their
eyes, and they saw that they were inside Samaria. When the king
of Israel saw them he said to Elisha, 'Father, shall I kill them? Shall
I kill them?' He answered, 'No! Did you capture with your sword
and your bow those whom you want to kill? Set food and water
before them so that they may eat and drink; and let them go to
their master.' So he prepared for them a great feast; after they ate
and drank, he sent them on their way, and they went to their
master. And the Arameans no longer came raiding into the land of
Israel.

2 KINGS 6:15–23

The Old Testament books of 1 and 2 Kings describe the history of Israel's monarchy from the closing days of the rule of King David (c.1000BC) until the time of the Babylonian exile (c.600BC).

Before the exile, two great prophets, Elijah and Elisha, rose up in the northern kingdom of Israel. Under King Ahab and Queen Jezebel, the people of Israel were worshipping the Phoenician fertility gods and turning their backs on the Lord. Elisha was the disciple and successor of Elijah, who, in his turn, engaged in the life-and-death struggle against these false gods.

Elijah was a rugged figure. Stern, authoritative and solitary, he also had great courage. He confronted King Ahab face to face before fleeing for his life (1 Kings 18). During his subsequent ministry, he raised the dead, healed the sick, and was fed by ravens in the wilderness.

Elisha's ministry was less confrontational and more concerned with the well-being of others, and the Bible records 18 encounters between Elisha and needy people. There was one famous occasion, however, when, taunted by some boys for being a 'baldhead', he cursed them in the name of the Lord: 'Then two she-bears came out of the woods and mauled forty-two of the boys' (2 Kings 2:24). According to some scholars, these victims were not children, but a mob of young men who, because they were from Bethel, the religious centre of idolatry, were probably warning Elisha not to speak against their practices as Elijah had done.

Elisha often lived with groups of other prophets and pursued his mission by working miracles. He was the son of a farmer in the Jordan valley, south of the sea of Galilee. One day, he was ploughing a field with a wooden plough pulled by oxen when the noted prophet Elijah came up and threw his cloak over him (1 Kings 19:19). Thus, his ministry began.

When Elijah's life and ministry on earth were over, he was dramatically carried up to heaven in a fiery chariot drawn by blazing horses. After witnessing this phenomenon, Elisha picked up his master's fallen cloak and with it the responsibility for his ministry, so that other prophets would say, 'The spirit of Elijah rests on Elisha' (2 Kings 2:15).

Elisha's final request to his mentor, on learning that the Lord was to take him away, had been, 'Please let me inherit a double share of your spirit' (v. 9). This was granted, and Elisha performed many miracles subsequently. He cleansed a foul stream by throwing in a handful of salt; at a time of famine, he made palatable a stew made of poisonous yellow gourds; he helped a destitute widow by making sure her meagre supply of saleable oil never ran out. More spectacularly, he raised a boy from the dead, again following in the footsteps of his master Elijah. Finding the boy lying dead on his bed, Elisha went in and closed the door and began to pray. He then lay down on the boy, breathing life into his mouth, and placing his hands upon his hands until the boy's flesh grew warm (4:32–37).

In spite of his ability to perform miracles, Elisha needed the protection of guardian angels, because the times he lived in were dangerous, with wars raging all around. In the passage from 2 Kings 6 at the start of this chapter, it seems that Elisha's army was very weak. In the hill town of Dothan, they were challenged by the king of Syria, who sent horses and chariots and a strong force that came by night and surrounded the city.

As he dressed in the morning, Elisha's servant saw to his horror that the surrounding hills were full of invaders. When he told Elisha, however, he realized that his master did not share his fears, as we can see by Elisha's reply: 'Do not be afraid, for there are more with us than there are with them' (v. 16). Then Elisha prayed that the servant's eyes would be opened. The prayer was answered, and he saw that 'the mountain was full of horses and chariots of fire all around Elisha' (v. 17).

Elisha was not only encouraged by the evidence of his own eyes. He wanted his servant to see the amazing sight of the army of guardian angels too, and God answered his prayer. Once the Syrian army was captured, he ordered that they be given food and water and then let go to return to their master. Elisha knew that it was the living God of Israel and his mighty army of angels that had saved the day. He wanted to give God honour, just as, in an earlier time, old

Abraham had shown his thankfulness by building altars to the Lord. Consciously or subconsciously, Elisha was also following the advice set out in the book of Proverbs: 'If your enemies are hungry, give them bread to eat; and if they are thirsty, give them water to drink; for you will heap coals of fire on their heads, and the Lord will reward you' (25:21–22).

Elisha's act of clemency bore fruit in a temporary truce in the fighting. For a while, at least, the Syrians no longer came raiding into the land of Israel, whose God had been proved once again to be all-powerful, and also all-merciful.

Powerful guardian angels appear in the book of Psalms, that wonderful collection of poetry, attributed in part to King David, which has inspired God's people for thousands of years. Probably the most well-known and inspiring angelic passage comes from Psalm 91:11–13: 'For he will command his angels concerning you to guard you in all your ways. On their hands they will bear you up, so that you will not dash your foot against a stone. You will tread on the lion and the adder, the young lion and the serpent you will trample underfoot.' These words were even quoted by the devil when he came to tempt Jesus in the wilderness (Luke 4:10–11). The depiction of angels protecting those who tread and trample on snakes is a very powerful one, which is accepted by most scholars as poetic imagery. There are, however, still churches in the southern USA where the practice of handling deadly snakes persists as part of worship.

The work of guardian angels obviously includes disposing of enemies, and King David's response to being on the battlefield was to write Psalm 35. David calls for the angel of the Lord to protect him by vanquishing them: 'Let them be like chaff before the wind, with the angel of the Lord driving them on. Let their way be dark and slippery, with the angel of the Lord pursuing them' (vv. 5–6).

Like many of the heroes of the Old Testament, David lived a less than exemplary life. As well as being a great king and the ancestor of Jesus, he was an adulterer, murderer and liar. The Bible makes no attempt to hide David's failings, but God had looked into his very heart and known him as the chosen and soon-to-be-anointed king of Israel: 'for the Lord does not see as mortals see; they look on the outward appearance, but the Lord looks on the heart' (1 Samuel 16:7).

On his deathbed, David referred to himself as 'Israel's singer of songs' (2 Samuel 23:1, NIV). All his life, despite his sins, he had known himself to be in close communion with God and his guardian angels. A man who lived with great zest, he was always quick to confess his sins, but he never took God's forgiveness lightly or his blessing for granted. Many of his Psalms, though not mentioning guardian angels by name, do assure us of God's continuing love and protection: 'I keep the Lord always before me; because he is at my right hand, I shall not be moved' (Psalm 16:8).

A guardian angel appears in the story of Shadrach, Meshach and Abednego (Daniel 1:6–7; 3:1–30), which is set in the period following the siege and capture of Jerusalem by King Nebuchadnezzar of Babylon (c.605BC). The three young Hebrews had been brought to the Babylonian court, along with their friend Daniel, to serve in the king's palace and be taught the literature and language of the Chaldeans. They were to be educated for three years so that at the end of that time they could be stationed in the king's court.

Unfortunately, this education included paying homage to a golden statue, made by King Nebuchadnezzar, which Shadrach, Meshach and Abednego vigorously refused to do. They were given precise instructions by the king himself on how this homage must be paid to the accompaniment of a great musical fanfare. If the three young men refused to fall down and worship the golden statue, they would immediately be thrown into a terrible, blazing furnace (3:15).

Even though threatened with this horrific death, Shadrach, Meshach and Abednego defied the king to his face: 'If our God whom we serve is able to deliver us from the furnace of blazing fire and out of your hand, O king, let him deliver us. But if not, be it known to you, O king, that we will not serve your gods and we will not worship the golden statue that you have set up' (vv. 17–18).

In a fury, the king ordered the furnace to be heated to seven times its usual intensity, so that the men who threw the young captives into the flames were themselves burnt to death. But to the king's amazement, Daniel's friends were joined in the furnace by a guardian angel, who protected them from the flames: 'I see four men unbound, walking in the middle of the fire, and they are not hurt; and the fourth has the appearance of a god,' Nebuchadnezzar exclaimed (v. 25). He went to the door of the furnace and called the young men out, and when they were examined it was found that they were completely unscathed, without a hair of their heads singed, or their tunics tainted by the smell of smoke (v. 27).

Nebuchadnezzar was so astonished that he blessed the God of Shadrach, Meshach and Abednego, who had so wonderfully repaid their trust. His joy in his own encounter with God and his angel seems to have been boundless, because Nebuchadnezzar made a decree that any people, nation or language that uttered blasphemy against God should be torn limb from limb, and their houses laid in ruins, 'for there is no other god who is able to deliver in this way' (v. 29). The intervention of a guardian angel resulted in Shadrach, Meshach and Abednego being promoted in the province of Babylon, where, though still in exile, they continued to serve their God faithfully.

Such service in a hostile environment was not without its traumas and tribulations, however, and in Daniel 6 we read the well-known account of how Daniel himself was thrown into the lions' den in the court of King Darius. Jealous of Daniel's success and royal patronage, his rivals persuaded the king to pass a decree forbidding the worship of any god except himself for a period of a month. Daniel, however, continued to kneel in daily prayer to the God of his fathers. When this was reported to the king, Darius saw that he had been tricked, but his nobles insisted that the law, which could not now be altered, demanded that Daniel be thrown to the lions. The story goes on, painting vivid and dramatic scenes:

Then the king gave the command, and Daniel was brought and thrown into the den of lions. The king said to Daniel, 'May your God, whom you faithfully serve, deliver you!' A stone was brought and laid on the mouth of the den, and the king sealed it with his own signet and with the signet of his lords, so that nothing might be changed concerning Daniel. Then the king went to his palace and spent the night fasting; no food was brought to him, and sleep fled from him. Then, at break of day, the king got up and hurried to the den of lions. When he came near the den where Daniel was, he cried out anxiously to Daniel, 'O Daniel, servant of the living God, has your God whom you faithfully serve been able to deliver you from the lions?' Daniel then said to the king, 'O king, live for ever! My God sent his angel and shut the lions' mouths so that they would not hurt me, because I was found blameless before him; and also before you, O king, I have done no wrong.'

DANIEL 6:16–22

Reluctant as he had been to consign the young Israelite to such a violent death, Darius was glad to rejoice with him. In fact, the king, like Nebuchadnezzar, felt moved to make a royal decree, but his was much more explicit and spiritually joyful. He ordered that in all of his land, people should do more than respect the God of Daniel: they should 'tremble and fear' before him (v. 26). Darius acknowledged the sovereignty and power of the God whom he now recognized as not only living, but living for ever. This great king could find it within himself to offer the highest praise for God's mighty works of delivery and rescue, and his signs and wonders both in heaven and on earth, 'for he has saved Daniel from the power of the lions' (v. 27).

It is becoming clear that guardian angels appear in the Old Testament when there is great danger. They are also involved when God gives a seemingly impossible task to a human who is convinced of their own weakness and ineptitude. In a story set around the time of the battle of Jericho, a strange man with a drawn sword suddenly appeared to Joshua before he was given the specific instructions that resulted in the fall of the impenetrable walls of the great city. 'As commander of the army of the Lord I have now come,' the man said (Joshua 5:14). In an echo of Moses' instructions at the burning bush, the man also ordered Joshua to remove the sandals from his feet, 'for the place where you stand is holy' (v. 15).

Long before, and on his deathbed, Jacob, whose message from a ladder of angels had changed his life, blessed his grandsons. In so doing, he told them of another angel—the guardian who had protected him over many years: 'The angel who has redeemed me from all harm, bless the boys; and in them let my name be perpetuated, and the name of my ancestors Abraham and Isaac; and let them grow into a multitude on the earth' (Genesis 48:16).

Jacob was surely remembering the time when he actually wrestled with an angel. On his way to meet his brother Esau after many years' separation, he was met by the angels of God (Genesis 32:1), and when Jacob saw them, he said, 'This is God's camp!' (v. 2). He called that place 'Mahanaim', meaning 'two camps' (presumably of earth and heaven). Jacob was overcome with shame at the way, as an impetuous young man, he had tricked and mistreated his brother. He prayed to the God of his fathers that Esau would forgive him and spare his life, so that he could return to the country and kindred where God had told him he belonged.

The night before he came face to face with his brother, a man suddenly appeared in front of him. In this strange story, the Bible tells us that the man wrestled with Jacob all through the night, and eventually struck him on the hip socket so that Jacob's hip was put out of joint. As day was breaking, and the stranger asked that he might leave, Jacob requested a blessing. On giving his name, he was told, 'You shall no longer be called Jacob, but Israel, for you have striven with God and with humans, and have prevailed' (v. 28). Jacob then asked the wrestler to identify himself. He received no reply, but he did get his requested blessing. Jacob called the place 'Peniel', meaning 'face of God'. He declared, 'For I have seen God face to face, and yet my life is preserved' (v. 30)

Jacob's whole life was changed by this strange incident. Now that he had finally acknowledged God as the source of all his blessings, God was able to reveal part of his plan for Jacob's life in his service, a plan that, like the one involving his grandfather Abraham, required a change of name. Jacob had been chosen to be the father of the twelve tribes of Israel. His story was passed down, at first verbally, through the generations. Many years later, the prophet Hosea spoke of his ancestor Jacob: 'He strove with the angel and prevailed, he wept and sought his favour' (Hosea 12:4).

The Bible tells us that God's guardian angels are part of a mighty army. They appear in force in the scriptures when God's people are in mortal danger, as in Elisha's battle experience. But they also come, when needed, as individuals to individuals, to save and rescue, or just to assure us of their presence, however unexpected or challenging that presence may be.

When they are recognized, as in the case of Jacob, the knowledge of their holy support gives wisdom and direction where only greed and folly may have existed before. King David's awareness of mighty guardian angels was essential to his heartfelt songs of thanks and praise, as well as being part of dire warnings to his enemies. To Daniel and his Hebrew friends, Shadrach, Meshach and Abednego, the angel of the Lord was one who could shut the mouth of a ravenous lion and also walk through flames, a shining one with the appearance of a god. He even changed the minds of the most powerful of heathen kings.

6

GUARDIANS IN THE
NEW TESTAMENT

At that time the disciples came to Jesus and asked. 'Who is the greatest in the kingdom of heaven?' He called a child, whom he put among them, and said, 'Truly I tell you, unless you change and become like children, you will never enter the kingdom of heaven. Whoever becomes humble like this child is the greatest in the kingdom of heaven. Whoever welcomes one such child in my name welcomes me.

'If any of you put a stumbling block before one of these little ones who believe in me, it would be better for you if a great millstone were fastened around your neck and you were drowned in the depth of the sea. Woe to the world because of stumbling-blocks! Occasions for stumbling are bound to come, but woe to the one by whom the stumbling block comes!

'If your hand or your foot causes you to stumble, cut it off and throw it away; it is better for you to enter life maimed or lame than to have two hands or two feet and to be thrown into the eternal fire. And if your eye causes you to stumble, tear it out and throw it away; it is better for you to enter life with one eye than to have two eyes and to be thrown into the hell of fire.

'Take care that you do not despise one of these little ones; for, I tell you, in heaven their angels continually see the face of my Father in heaven. What do you think? If a shepherd has a hundred sheep, and one of them has gone astray, does he not leave the ninety-nine on the mountains and go in search of the one that went astray? And if he finds it, truly I tell you, he rejoices over it

more than over the ninety-nine that never went astray. So it is not the will of your Father in heaven that one of these little ones should be lost.'
MATTHEW 18:1–14

In Jesus' time and culture, children, like women, were unimportant nonentities, who had no voice in society. Infant mortality was fairly high, and although grown-up children were useful to care for their parents in old age, their significance while growing would have been questionable to most of the people listening to Jesus that day.

This is a typical example in which Jesus turned completely upside down the inherited knowledge by which people unquestioningly lived their lives. Even the disciples must have been astonished when Jesus put a child in the middle of their group and explained that having a child's humility was necessary in order to gain the kingdom of heaven.

But Jesus went even further with both a radical announcement, 'Whoever welcomes one such child in my name welcomes me' (v. 5), and a chilling warning, 'If any of you put a stumbling-block before one of these little ones who believe in me, it would be better for you if a great millstone were fastened around your neck and you were drowned in the depth of the sea' (v. 6). Children are so special to his Father, Jesus went on, that they have their own heavenly guardian angels: 'Take care that you do not despise one of these little ones; for, I tell you, in heaven their angels continually see the face of my Father in heaven' (v. 10). This is a very comforting thought, and there are many Christians of all denominations who believe that the personal angel protector assigned to them at birth stays with them throughout their life on earth.

Jesus' earthly father, Joseph, was addressed at least twice by an angel of the Lord who, intent upon guarding the infant Jesus' life, appeared to Joseph in dreams. The first time was after the visit of the wise men who came from the east, bearing gifts.

Now after they had left, an angel of the Lord appeared to Joseph in a dream and said, 'Get up, take the child and his mother, and flee to Egypt, and remain there until I tell you; for Herod is about to search for the child, to destroy him.' Then Joseph got up, took the child and his mother by night, and went to Egypt, and remained there until the death of Herod.
MATTHEW 2:13–15a

The second time Joseph dreamt and saw the angel, he was told that it was safe to return to his homeland.

When Herod died, an angel of the Lord suddenly appeared in a dream to Joseph in Egypt and said, 'Get up, take the child and his mother, and go to the land of Israel, for those who were seeking the child's life are dead.' Then Joseph got up, took the child and his mother, and went to the land of Israel. But when he heard that Archelaus was ruling over Judea in place of his father Herod, he was afraid to go there. And after being warned in a dream, he went away to the district of Galilee. There he made his home in a town called Nazareth.
MATTHEW 2:19–23a

In 1 Corinthians 4:9, Paul says we are a 'spectacle' to the angels—an image that brings to my mind a scene from the film *City of Angels* (1998), in which clusters of darkly clad angels inhabit the tops of tall buildings, watching unseen the busy lives of human beings. Their closeness as depicted in the film is both strange and comforting, drawing on the instinctive feeling that most of us have had from time to time that we are 'not alone'.

In the early Christian church, angels were used by God to protect the followers of Jesus. After he ascended into heaven and the disciples received the promised gift of the Holy Spirit at Pentecost, the church grew quickly: 'Day by day, as they spent much time together in the temple, they broke bread at home and ate their food with glad and generous hearts, praising God and having the goodwill of all the people. And day by day the Lord added to their number those who were being saved' (Acts 2:46–47).

As Jesus himself had prophesied, however, the church was also soon being persecuted. During this time, when many wonders and miraculous signs were done by the apostles, Peter healed a crippled beggar. He and John were taken before the Sanhedrin, the ruling Jewish court. They were placed in custody overnight, but the court could not decide how to punish them because all the people were praising God for the healing that had happened.

Eventually, the two apostles were released, with dire warnings not to speak to anyone in the name of Jesus—but this was impossible for them to do. Peter and John were emboldened by the Holy Spirit, and determined to speak in the name of their risen and ascended Lord. Not surprisingly, before long, they were arrested again and put in the public jail. It was then, as Luke tells us in Acts 5, that they received a welcome but unexpected visitor: 'During the night an angel of the Lord opened the prison doors, brought them out, and said, "Go, stand in the temple and tell the people the whole message about this life." When they heard this, they entered the temple at daybreak and went on with their teaching' (vv. 19–21).

The book of Acts is alive with adventure, and with angels. The first martyr, Stephen, defending his faith to his grim-faced murderers, described the angel who had appeared to Moses in the middle of the burning bush (7:30–38); and an angel of the Lord appeared to Philip, guiding him as he began his evangelistic ministry among the Gentiles (8:26). An avenging angel eventually struck down Herod, who had already had James, the brother of John, killed with the sword, and Peter imprisoned. Herod was more interested in giving self-important speeches than in paying proper homage to God: 'And immediately, because he had not given the glory to God, an angel of the Lord struck him down, and he was eaten by worms and died' (12:23).

In Acts 12, before the death of Herod, we read of Peter again being imprisoned. There were four squads of soldiers stationed to keep him there, but the church was praying fervently for him. The night he was due to appear before Herod, probably to be condemned to death, Peter, bound with two chains, was sleeping between two soldiers.

Suddenly an angel of the Lord appeared and a light shone in the cell. He tapped Peter on the side and woke him, saying, 'Get up quickly.' And the chains fell off his wrists. The angel said to him, 'Fasten your belt and put on your sandals.' He did so. Then he said to him, 'Wrap your cloak around you and follow me.' Peter went out and followed him; he did not realize that what was happening with the angel's help was real; he thought he was seeing a vision. After they had passed the first and the second guard, they came before the iron gate leading into the city. It opened for them of its own accord, and they went outside and walked along a lane, when suddenly the angel left him. Then Peter came to himself and said, 'Now I am sure that the Lord has sent his angel and rescued me from the hands of Herod and from all that the Jewish people were expecting.'
ACTS 12:7–11

In the garden of Gethsemane, following his betrayal and arrest, Jesus said, 'Do you think that I cannot appeal to my Father, and he will at once send me more than twelve legions of angels?' (Matthew 26:53). It seems clear from this that he could have had a whole army of personal angelic bodyguards at his disposal. Yet he did not call upon them to save him from the death he knew he had to suffer, for our sakes, on the cross. He went on to say, 'But how then would the scriptures be fulfilled, which say it must happen in this way?' (v. 54). In the same way, Jesus had also refused the protection of angels when reminded of them by Satan, who tempted him in the wilderness: 'Then the devil took him to the holy city and placed him on the pinnacle of the temple, saying to him, "If you are the Son of God, throw yourself down; for it is written, 'He will command his angels concerning you', and 'On their hands they will bear you up, so that you will not dash your foot against a stone'"' (Matthew 4:5–6).

In the New Testament, guardian angels are shown to be on hand to protect the 'little ones' whom Jesus esteemed and identified with.

They guarded the baby Jesus by appearing to Joseph in warning dreams. Their promise persisted in the face of suffering, temptation and even martyrdom, and they ensured that the ministry of Jesus went on by arranging spectacular prison breakouts for those who could not help but speak his name.

7

GUARDIANS: PERSONAL
EXPERIENCES

On the evening of 24 April 1996, Mark and I were walking down a dirt road in Konjra, in the wilds of western Kenya. Around us were dwellings made of mud and straw, and the road was full of Kenyans of all ages and sizes, walking barefoot, stopping to greet each other and us with the familiar, heart-warming words, *'Bwana Asifiwe!'* ('Praise the Lord').

We were in Kenya for only three months, working as chaplains at the Metropolitan hospital, Buru-Buru, near Nairobi, but we had immediately seen the contrast between this world and our own comfortable one in the West. In this isolated rural area, people were striving just to survive, and as we walked, accompanied by a local Anglican priest, we passed sellers of sugar cane and bananas, seated on the dusty ground. Women, bent almost horizontal with loads of maize on their backs, moved by in the strange light that came before the sudden darkness of the African night, and children, some as young as six or seven, carried petrol cans filled with drinking water on their heads.

'Don't they realize the dangers of lead poisoning?' I asked, horrified.

The Revd Nick shook his head. 'Many things in the West are taken for granted,' he said, 'but people here really do not know that contaminated water can be dangerous. We still have typhoid because it is not known that water should be boiled, and not taken from near latrines.'

As he spoke, we turned a corner in the road, and there was a tiny stall, half hidden in the undergrowth and made entirely from an overturned wooden box.

'*Jambo!*' We stopped and shook hands with the teenage girl who stood alone behind the box.

'Here is your local supermarket, sister Carol!' Nick joked. He introduced us to the girl. 'These people are two pastors from England.'

I looked down at the stall, seeing the usual pitiful assortment of items: candles, matches, pencil stubs, a block of Kimbo cooking fat, cut into two-ounce pieces. Just then, a small boy appeared at my elbow. Holding out a coin, he pointed to the block of fat. The girl took his money and wrapped a precious square of Kimbo in a piece of newspaper that she took from a dusty cardboard box at the back of the stall. Mosquitoes buzzed around our heads.

'Don't go yet, *bwana!*' As we prepared to leave, the girl held out a restraining hand and turned back to the box. To my surprise, she took from it a battered Bible and a piece of paper. 'You may be able to help me,' she said. 'All day, I have been looking for a quotation. It is for my Sunday school test.'

In the fading light, we all peered at the pencilled question: 'Where is it that Jesus says, "In heaven, their angels continually see the face of my Father in heaven"?'

At my side, Mark smiled. 'That's Matthew 18, verse 10.' Reaching across, he took the Bible and turned its pages. 'There, look, it's where he's talking to the disciples about not despising the little children.'

The girl thanked us and we turned to go on our way. As we did so, I suddenly became aware of another group of trudging people, only half visible on the broad, pot-holed path. A woman, accompanied by several children, was walking on her way to some unknown bushland destination. As Nick called out a greeting, she stopped, and the eldest child, a girl of about eight, stopped too. Her left leg was extended painfully in front of her, and blood and pus were running down it on to her filthy bare foot.

'What have you done?' Imagining it to be the result of some recent fall or accident, I hurried to her side.

The child just looked at me, her dark eyes mute and full of suffering. I turned to Nick. 'Please, ask her mother how she has done this.'

Looking down at her leg, I saw a huge, livid wound, open to the bone, stretching from her knee all the way down her shin. Nick spoke quickly to the woman, who was staring suspiciously at us, her three other children clinging to her skirts.

After a moment's conversation, Nick told us, 'She says it just came. Sometimes these things are a result of malnutrition,' he went on, as the woman, indicating for the child to walk ahead, slid away into the darkness. 'A simple bite or burn, when the body has no resistance and conditions are unhygienic, can turn into a killer.'

We carried on towards our own destination in silence, all of us thinking of what we had seen. When at last we reached Nick's house, where we were staying, Mark turned to me. 'Strange,' he mused, 'about that scripture reading. It came just before we turned and saw her.'

'Nick!' How slow we are sometimes, and how tired God our Father must be of nudging us into action! It was so obvious that we had been reminded of the special place of children in God's kingdom, and here we were, just walking away from a child whose suffering we surely could alleviate. I reached out for Nick's arm. 'We must find out who that little girl is!' I urged. 'Will you promise to find her for me tomorrow?'

Well, thanks to the Revd Nick Adjuoga and the efforts of a lot of other people, both in Kenya and back in our parish in England, the girl, Patricia Auma, was able to get the treatment she needed, and a clinic was eventually set up to help others like her in rural Konjra. We didn't see her guardian angel, but he was certainly on duty that night, and just to remember the 'coincidence' of the reading and then Patricia's sudden appearance on that road still makes me catch my breath in wonder.

Ann Walters is an Anglican priest, serving here in the Black Country. She told me, 'I actually saw my son's guardian angel. Martin was about twelve years old at the time, but thought he was much older. At school, he'd been labelled dyslexic and attention-deficient, and he was always in trouble. I worried continually that something terrible would happen to him—that my husband and I weren't able to do enough to protect him.

'One night, we had a violent row. We were due to go to a family party, but Martin threw a wobbly and said he didn't want to go. Before we could stop him, he'd stormed out of the house. It was a dark winter's night, and I was really scared. I ran out after him, but he was nowhere in sight, so I went upstairs and looked through the window. I still couldn't see Martin. But then I noticed a tall man, standing really still under the lamp-post, as if he were waiting for someone. When Martin did appear, coming from the back of his friend's house, the man left the lamp-post and began to follow him, close behind.'

Ann broke off, tears filling her eyes. 'I was petrified. "There's a man following Martin!" I told my husband as I ran down the stairs. Through my mind were going all the things you read in the papers about kids being abducted and murdered—and my twelve-year-old son was out there with somebody stalking him! We both ran into the street, round the back of the houses. There was no sign of Martin or the strange man. I was frantic, and Paul was really worried too. But as we looked at each other, wondering what to do next, someone called, and our son was suddenly there, coming back home, quite safe and all on his own.

'"Hadn't we better get ready for this party, then?" he asked, cheekily. All his bad temper had gone! When I asked him, carefully, about the man I had seen walking so closely and quietly behind him a few minutes earlier, Martin frowned. "I didn't see anybody, Mum," he insisted. "There was nobody there!"

'Martin didn't see or hear anybody, even though the man was walking so near to him,' Ann finished. 'He and his father think I imagined it. But I know now that my son does have a guardian angel, and even though he still has his problems, I'll never be so worried about him in quite the same way again.'

Visible guardian angels are not as far-fetched as we may think.

There are many well-documented accounts of people experiencing their special protection in times of danger or crisis.

In her book, *Where Angels Walk*, Joan Wester Anderson describes several incidents that cannot be explained in everyday, logical terms. One is about a family threatened by thugs on motorbikes, who suddenly gave up and drove away as fast as they could. The father had been holding his camera, and when the film was developed, a white-clad angel could be clearly seen, standing guard over the threatened family.

Another incident Anderson cites is of a young woman walking home from work through Brooklyn, who suddenly became aware that a man was following her. 'Stacey had an immediate feeling of fear; there had been some recent muggings in the neighbourhood, and she sensed the man was up to no good. But she had no choice—the only way to her apartment was to pass him. "Guardian angel, protect me," Stacey murmured. "Be right beside me now and save me from harm."'

Next day, on her way to work, Stacey learnt that there had been a rape in the district, just after the time she had passed the man. She went to the police, where she learnt that they had someone in custody, and was invited to take part in an identity parade.

Stacey agreed. That night she identified him as the man she had passed on her way home. 'Why didn't he attack me?' she asked the policeman. 'After all, I was just as vulnerable as the next woman who came along.' The policeman was curious too, and he agreed to describe Stacey to the suspect and ask him if he remembered her. Stacey never forgot his answer: 'I remember her. But why would I have bothered her?' the rapist asked. 'She was walking down the street with two big guys, one on either side of her.' [3]

Reports of guardian angels also appear in historical accounts. There have been reports written at various times that seem to bear witness to their existence. Perhaps the most famous of these stories concerns the 'Angel of Mons', which appeared during a critical period in World War I. *The Observer* newspaper, on 22 August 1915, carried a report that a soldier in a military hospital had told a nurse that during the British retreat from Mons, Belgium (August 1914), a luminous angel with outstretched wings came between the Germans and themselves. At that moment, the onslaught of the enemy slackened.[4]

In the same year, *The Universe* newspaper carried an officer's letter that told of a party of 30 men cut off in a trench. In order to avoid being trapped, they decided to make a sortie against the enemy. As they ran out, they became aware of a large company of men going along with them, leading them towards the enemy trenches. Afterwards, the officer talked with a prisoner whom they had captured. The prisoner asked a very strange question: 'Who was that soldier on a great white horse who led you? Although he was so prominent, none of our men were able to hit him!'

There seems to be a clear comparison here with the account in 2 Kings when Elisha and his servant were given the ability to see God's hosts of guardian-angel fighters all around. Guardian angels appear when they are most needed, and there are accounts from World War II that correspond with the Angel of Mons stories. The *South London Newspaper* reported, on 8 September 1944, that an angel was seen in the sky during an air raid on Peckham. In another incident, during the same war, a man who was tending his sheep on the Sussex Downs noticed a white line spreading slowly across the sky. As the man stared at it, the apparition gradually took the shape of Christ on the cross, with six angels appearing beside him. There were several other witnesses to this strange phenomena, which lasted for several minutes. One of them described the angels graphically, and said that they appeared to be praying.

Although some people might dismiss these accounts as the by-product of the traumas of war, it is possible, through faith, to see them as proof that guardian angels are always on hand, ready to fly to our defence at times of greatest trial. This sentiment is supported by a story told by the Revd Wallace Brown and his wife Mary, who moved with their family to serve in an inner-city parish in a rough part of Birmingham. In recent years, the vicarage garden had been invaded nightly by a gang of youths who threw bottles, left contraceptives, and defaced everything in sight, including the church noticeboard, with knives. The Browns feared not only for their own safety but for that of their young daughter, Elizabeth.

In desperation, Mary sat up all through one night, seeking God's guidance in what seemed like a no-win situation. Her prayers led her to the Old Testament book of Nehemiah, which tells the story of the rebuilding of the walls of Jerusalem during the time of exile following the city's fall in 587BC. Called by God to rebuild the walls, the prophet Nehemiah, who worked as a cupbearer to the king of Babylon, spent time weeping, fasting and mourning before he asked for permission to return to Jerusalem to fulfil his seemingly impossible task.

When he arrived in the city, Nehemiah found that groups of raiders had captured the walls. Nehemiah was undeterred: 'So we rebuilt the wall, and all the wall was joined together to half its height; for the people had a mind to work' (4:6). As enemies saw the gaps in the walls being closed, they became angry and threatening, but again Nehemiah's confidence was unshaken: 'So we prayed to our God, and set a guard as a protection against them day and night' (v. 9).

The Browns had no physical guards to place on their garden walls in Birmingham. Their congregation was small and elderly and naturally nervous of physical conflict. But in answer to their prayers, God gave Mary and Wallace an understanding that he would place guardian angels there. They were to pray for this protection every day, and to continue to pray, as Nehemiah had. Wallace reports, 'The very next day, Mary and I went out and prayed "on location". Feeling slightly foolish, I asked God to place guardian angels all around the walls, to make them safe, and to bring godliness to our lawns and boundaries. It felt good.'[5]

Over the next few days, to Wallace and Mary's astonishment, the gang of 35 screaming and swearing youths decreased to about ten. Each day, the Browns went out and prayed that God would keep his guardian angels around the vicarage garden walls. By the end of the following week, the number of youths they encountered had dropped to a mere two or three. The relief at the break-up of the gang that had terrorized the whole neighbourhood meant freedom not only for the vicarage family but for others who now felt able to come to church again. The Browns conclude, 'After year upon year of human failure, the terrible "siege" of church and vicarage was broken by the supernatural holy presence of God's angels.'

The Browns' experience reminds me of our own dilemma when moving into our present vicarage at Short Heath. Empty for two years after the last incumbent had left, it was invaded by squatters, who daubed obscene graffiti on the bedroom walls and finally trashed the place, causing £20,000 worth of damage. 'They've pulled all the ceilings down, smashed the toilets with a hammer, kicked holes in the doors, and they must've found a tin of paint. That's been thrown all over the wooden floors!' Mark told me over the phone on the morning he was due to meet the decorators in the house. 'Will you ring the diocesan housing officer while I wait for the police?'

Barry, the housing officer, was shocked when I repeated Mark's description of the damage. He said he would get to the house as soon as possible. I rang Mark's mobile to tell him to wait. It was engaged, and so, on impulse, I rang a friend and told her what had happened. 'Just pray for some protection!' I begged. 'We've been so looking forward to the new job, and although the vicarage needed cleaning up, it looked perfect for our ministry there.'

'I'll ask for nine-foot angels!' Noreen promised, before I rang off. 'Everything will be fine. Wait and see. Just trust in the Lord!'

'Trust in the Lord.' I thought of the words as I tried Mark's number again. This time he answered, and I told him what the housing officer had said.

'Barry's just rung to say he's on his way,' Mark said, sounding surprised. 'And I can hardly believe this, but he's also said he's decided to get a private security firm in here. They'll patrol three times a day with a dog, from when the workmen start until we move in. It'll cost the diocese a packet, but it'll be worth it to know the place is safe!'

'Would the patrol have wings?' I wondered privately, as I thought about Noreen's angels, nine feet high! But all I said was, 'Thank you, Barry!' and, under my breath, 'Thanks, Lord!'

✤

You come through thick stone walls, armed guards and bars; you bring me a starry night and ask about this and that. You are the Redeemer. I recognize you. You are my way, my truth and my life. Even my cellar blooms with stars, and peace and light pour forth. You sprinkle beautiful words on me like flowers: 'Son, what are you afraid of? I am with you.'
VIKTORUS PETKUS (b. 1929)

> *But now, thus says the Lord,*
> *he who created you, O Jacob,*
> *he who formed you, O Israel:*
> *Do not fear, for I have redeemed you;*
> *I have called you by name, you are mine.*
> *When you pass through the waters, I will be with you;*
> *and through the rivers, they shall not overwhelm you.*
> ISAIAH 43:1–2

Heavenly Father, we thank you for the guardian angels who protect us day by day. We ask your special protection for all who are in dangerous situations throughout this troubled world, especially Christians who are being killed and persecuted for their faith. Amen.

—————— *8* ——————

MINISTERING ANGELS
IN THE OLD TESTAMENT

Ahab told Jezebel all that Elijah had done, and how he had killed all the prophets with the sword. Then Jezebel sent a message to Elijah, saying, 'So may the gods do to me, and more also, if I do not make your life like the life of one of them by this time tomorrow.' Then he was afraid; he got up and fled for his life, and came to Beersheba, which belongs to Judah; he left his servant there.

But he himself went a day's journey into the wilderness, and came and sat down under a solitary broom tree. He asked that he might die: 'It is enough; now, O Lord, take away my life, for I am no better than my ancestors.' Then he lay down under the broom tree and fell asleep. Suddenly an angel touched him and said to him, 'Get up and eat.' He looked, and there at his head was a cake baked on hot stones, and a jar of water. He ate and drank, and lay down again. The angel of the Lord came a second time, touched him, and said, 'Get up and eat, otherwise the journey will be too much for you.' He got up, and ate and drank; then he went in the strength of that food for forty days and forty nights to Horeb the mount of God.

1 KINGS 19:1–8

The first book of Kings graphically describes an epic contest on Mount Carmel between the prophet Elijah and the priests and prophets of Baal. In this battle, Elijah challenged Baal's disciples to prepare an altar, complete with sacrifice, but without fire. He, too, built an altar, to the living God of Israel. The deity who responded to the call to send down fire would be deemed both authentic and mighty.

'So they took the bull that was given them, prepared it, and called on the name of Baal from morning until noon, crying, "O Baal, answer us!" But there was no voice, and no answer. They limped about the altar that they had made' (1 Kings 18:26). Even though the prophets cried aloud and, according to their worship customs, cut themselves with swords and lances until they were covered in blood, Baal did not send down fire. In fact, there was 'no voice, no answer, and no response' (v. 29).

Confidently, Elijah then invited all the people to move closer to him. First, he repaired an altar of the Lord that had previously been torn down. He set up twelve stones, one for each of the sons of Jacob. Then, after laying the altar with wood and the sacrifice, he ordered that four jars of water be emptied all over and around the altar, three times, so that even the trench surrounding it was brimming. Elijah then prayed aloud that all would be made aware of the power of the one true God, whom he served: 'Answer me, O Lord, answer me, so that this people may know that you, O Lord, are God, and that you have turned their hearts back' (v. 37).

His prayer was answered in a very dramatic way, because the fire of the Lord immediately came down and burnt the offering and the wood, then the stones and dust, and finally consumed even the water in the trench. 'When all the people saw it, they fell on their faces and said, "The Lord indeed is God; the Lord indeed is God"' (v. 39). Elijah ordered the prophets of Baal to be seized, emphasizing that not one of them must be allowed to escape. Then he put them all to death. It was not surprising that Elijah soon received a chilling message from Queen Jezebel, declaring that she would avenge the dead prophets of Baal by taking Elijah's life. She swore it colourfully and emphatically upon her own life.

Elijah was naturally terrified, and ran. In spite of his great triumph on Mount Carmel and the dramatic demonstration of the power of the living God, he knew the very real danger he was in.

Leaving his servant in Beersheba, he fled far into the wilderness and sat down under a solitary broom tree, a desert bush, and prayed that he might die as a happy release from all his troubles. Then he lay down under the tree and fell asleep, no doubt hoping that he would awake in heaven.

It was then that a ministering angel came to Elijah. The angel touched him and said, 'Get up and eat' (19:5). Elijah looked, and there at his head was a cake baked on hot stones, and a jar of water—a miracle indeed in such an isolated place. He ate and drank, glad to do as he had been told, and then lay down again. Then the angel came a second time and repeated the procedure, urging him to eat, 'otherwise the journey will be too much for you' (v. 7).

The food gave Elijah superhuman power. He went in the strength of it to Horeb, the sacred mountain, also known as Mount Sinai, where God had given his law to Moses. Elijah was still fearful: he hid in a cave, and complained to God about the impossibility of the tasks he was being given.

Then the word of the Lord came to him, saying, 'What are you doing here, Elijah?' He answered, 'I have been very zealous for the Lord, the God of hosts; for the Israelites have forsaken your covenant, thrown down your altars, and killed your prophets with the sword. I alone am left, and they are seeking my life, to take it away.'

He said, 'Go out and stand on the mountain before the Lord, for the Lord is about to pass by.' Now there was a great wind, so strong that it was splitting mountains and breaking rocks in pieces before the Lord, but the Lord was not in the wind; and after the wind an earthquake, but the Lord was not in the earthquake; and after the earthquake a fire, but the Lord was not in the fire; and after the fire a sound of sheer silence.
1 KINGS 19:9–12

God spoke to Elijah again after the sound of sheer silence, or, as it is sometimes translated, 'a still small voice'. The fierce and fearful prophet was reminded—just as he had been reminded through the ministry of the angel whom God had sent to feed him—that the owner of that 'still small voice' could be depended upon, no matter how the earthquake, wind and fire threatened, or Queen Jezebel raged.

There are several other places in the Old Testament where ministering angels are sent to sustain God's people with food and drink, very often when they have reached the point of starvation.

In the book of Genesis, Abram's wife Sarai suggested that he father a child with her Egyptian maidservant Hagar—a common practice in those times when polygamy was the norm and being barren was considered a terrible stigma. Hagar conceived, but before her son Ishmael was born, she ran away from Sarai, who had dealt harshly with her. There was understandable conflict between the two women, and Hagar was accused, rightly or wrongly, of looking on her barren mistress with contempt.

The angel of the Lord found Hagar in the wilderness, and advised her to go home. He passed on God's reassuring message about Ishmael's future.

The angel of the Lord said to her, 'Return to your mistress, and submit to her.' The angel of the Lord also said to her, 'I will so greatly multiply your offspring that they cannot be counted for multitude.' And the angel of the Lord said to her, 'Now you have conceived and shall bear a son; you shall call him Ishmael, for the Lord has given heed to your affliction. He shall be a wild ass of a man, with his hand against everyone, and everyone's hand against him; and he shall live at odds with all his kin.'
GENESIS 16:9–12

Consoled and encouraged by her spiritual encounter, Hagar was glad then to return to her mistress and to await the birth of her son. Once Sarah's own miraculous son Isaac was born, however, Abraham's wife found Hagar and her child Ishmael an embarrassment, and encouraged Abraham to cast them out. This was very distressing to Abraham, but God reassured him, telling him to do as Sarah said, because God had plans for Ishmael as well as for Isaac: 'for it is through Isaac that offspring shall be named after you. As for the son of the slave woman, I will make a nation of him also, because he is your offspring' (Genesis 21:12–13).

In spite of God's promises, Abraham must have had a heavy heart when, early on the appointed day, he gave Hagar bread and water and sent her away with her son. The extreme heat of the wilderness of Beersheba was enough to kill Hagar and her child, and her subsequent wanderings brought her near to the lairs of wild animals. When the water skin was empty, she put Ishmael under a bush and moved a distance away. She knew her baby was going to die, and she began to weep. Suddenly, the comforting voice of the angel of God called to her from heaven: 'What troubles you, Hagar? Do not be afraid; for God has heard the voice of the boy where he is. Come, lift up the boy and hold him fast with your hand, for I will make a great nation of him' (vv. 17–18). Then Hagar opened her eyes and saw a well of water. She went and filled her water skin and gave the boy a drink.

God was remembering the plans he had for Ishmael—plans to give him a future full of hope. Later in the chapter, we read, 'God was with the boy, and he grew up; he lived in the wilderness, and became an expert with the bow. He lived in the wilderness of Paran; and his mother got a wife for him from the land of Egypt' (v. 20). In fact, Ishmael became the leading patriarch for Islam, and he is still revered by Muslims today. In Islam, Ishmael is the favoured one, and he takes the place of Isaac in the narrative.

Abraham's other son Isaac knew the ministry of an angel in an even more dramatic way, when God tested Abraham to the very limit of his faith and love. In Genesis 22, we read how the Lord suddenly demanded that Abraham kill Isaac and offer him as a sacrifice on a rough-and-ready hilltop altar. Abraham was obedient, taking the young boy on a three-day trip that seemed destined to be Isaac's last. When they came to the place that God showed him, Abraham built an altar and laid the wood upon it. He bound Isaac, and laid him on top of the wood. Then he picked up the knife, preparing to kill him. It was then that the consoling voice of the ministering angel of the Lord called to Abraham from heaven: 'Do not lay your hand on the boy or do anything to him; for now I know that you fear God, since you have not withheld your son, your only son, from me' (v. 12).

Looking up, Abraham saw a ram, caught in a thicket by its horns: 'Abraham went and took the ram and offered it up as a burnt-offering instead of his son. So Abraham called that place "The Lord will provide"; as it is said to this day, "On the mount of the Lord it shall be provided"' (vv. 13–14).

It was then that the angel of the Lord called to Abraham again and told him that God had made a solemn oath. Because he had been prepared unquestioningly to sacrifice his promised and long-awaited son, God would bless him so abundantly that his descendants would be as numerous as the heavenly stars and earthly grains of sand: 'And your offspring shall possess the gate of their enemies, and by your offspring shall all the nations of the earth gain blessing for themselves, because you have obeyed my voice' (vv. 17–18).

Abraham's obedience showed that he still loved and trusted God implicitly. The angel who ministered to him and Isaac that day had a vital part to play. As well as words of comfort and prophecy, he provided the sacrificial ram—the equivalent, in that life-or-death situation, of Hagar's well of water and Elijah's cake made on hot stones.

The prophet Isaiah of Jerusalem was a counsellor to kings from 740 to 701 BC. During this time, there were two major crises: the war with Syria in 734 and the Assyrian threats from 734 to 701. In Isaiah 63:7–14, a later prophet in the school of Isaiah remembers God's mercy to the children of Israel and commends the Lord for being their saviour in all their times of distress. 'It was no messenger or angel but his presence that saved them,' Isaiah writes; '… he lifted them up and carried them all the days of old' (v. 9).

This is a timely reminder that behind each ministering angel there is the kindness and the command of our Father God, who, in his great love for the world and its fallen people, was more than prepared to go through the same ordeal that he ultimately spared his great friend Abraham. As Paul was to write many years later, 'He who did not withold his own Son, but gave him up for all of us, will he not with him also give us everything else?' (Romans 8:32).

---- *9* ----

MINISTERING ANGELS
IN THE NEW TESTAMENT

Then Jesus was led up by the Spirit into the wilderness to be tempted by the devil. He fasted for forty days and forty nights, and afterwards he was famished. The tempter came and said to him, 'If you are the Son of God, command these stones to become loaves of bread.' But he answered, 'It is written, "One does not live by bread alone, but by every word that comes from the mouth of God."'

Then the devil took him to the holy city and placed him on the pinnacle of the temple, saying to him, 'If you are the Son of God, throw yourself down; for it is written, "He will command his angels concerning you", and "On their hands they will bear you up, so that you will not dash your foot against a stone."' Jesus said to him, 'Again it is written, "Do not put the Lord your God to the test."'

Again, the devil took him to a very high mountain and showed him all the kingdoms of the world and their splendour; and he said to him, 'All these I will give you, if you will fall down and worship me.' Jesus said to him, 'Away with you, Satan! for it is written, "Worship the Lord your God, and serve only him."' Then the devil left him, and suddenly angels came and waited on him.

MATTHEW 4:1–11

At the start of his earthly ministry, after being baptized by John the Baptist in the river Jordan, Jesus fulfilled forty days and forty nights of desert fasting, just as the prophet Elijah had done after being fed by his ministering angel (1 Kings 19:8). Many, indeed, believed that Jesus might be a reincarnation of Elijah, a fact that was relayed by the disciples when he asked them, 'Who do people say that the Son of Man is?' (Matthew 16:13). In his time of fasting, however, Jesus was tempted by the devil—something that did not happen to Elijah.

The devil tempted him through his hunger, which must have been extreme ('If you are the Son of God, command these stones to become loaves of bread', Matthew 4:3). He tried spiritual testing, knowing that Jesus was, beneath his current distress, the glorious Son of God and more than entitled to his Father's supernatural protection ('Throw yourself down [from the temple]', v. 6). Finally, the devil tried to tempt Jesus with worldly wealth and power, something to which he himself had succumbed when, as Lucifer, he fell from God's grace ('All these I will give you, if you will fall down and worship me', v. 9).

Jesus resisted the devil—in fact, he sent him firmly away—but the place where he was stranded must have felt desolate and filled with a sense of foreboding. In some old illustrated Bibles, it is depicted as a barren rock, black and jagged, with no signs of vegetation or shelter. At his bleakest time, starving, thirsty and exhausted, half blinded beneath the desert sun, Jesus must have felt that God's angels were very far away from him. But when the devil eventually gave up and left him alone, we are told that they 'suddenly... came and waited on him' (v. 11).

His recognition of these ministering angels as familiar servants and allies must have gladdened Jesus' heart, because there is scriptural evidence that he was close to his Father's angels before his incarnation on this earth, and before and during his resurrection. An angel also ministered to him in those terrible moments in the garden of Gethsemane when he prayed in such anguish that his sweat became like drops of blood (Luke 22:43).

In the Gospel stories, Jesus is depicted as talking about the angels in an almost intimate way, as beings whom he knows and upon whom he can depend. He is able to describe how he saw the downfall of Satan: 'I watched Satan fall from heaven like a flash of lightning' (Luke 10:18). He can also say, when tested by religious leaders about the great father of faith, Abraham, 'Very truly, I tell you, before Abraham was, I am' (John 8:58). 'I am' was the holy name of God, imparted to Moses when the angel of the Lord appeared in the burning bush (Exodus 3:13–14). Not surprisingly, therefore, Jesus' listeners reacted violently to his words, picking up stones to throw at him, so that he had to hide himself and leave the temple.

We find further evidence of Jesus' knowledge of angels elsewhere in the Gospels. He knew, for instance, that there is joy in the presence of the angels of God over one sinner who repents (Luke 15:10). After calling Philip and Nathanael to be his disciples, Jesus promised Nathanael, 'Very truly, I tell you, you will see heaven opened and the angels of God ascending and descending upon the Son of Man' (John 1:51). This parallels Jacob's vision of a ladder full of angels in Genesis 28. Jesus also knew that angels 'neither marry nor are given in marriage' (Matthew 22:30), a fact that he could quote when tested in public by the Sadducees.

In the book of Ephesians we read about God's plan, which includes all Christ's followers and was perfected in heaven before time even began. It has Jesus at its core—truly the alpha and omega of all creation:

Blessed be the God and Father of our Lord Jesus Christ, who has blessed us in Christ with every spiritual blessing in the heavenly places, just as he chose us in Christ before the foundation of the world to be holy and blameless before him in love... With all wisdom and insight he has made known to us the mystery of his will, according to his good pleasure that he set forth in Christ, as a plan for the fullness of time, to gather up all things in him, things in heaven and things on earth.
EPHESIANS 1:3–4, 8–10

In his pre-existence, when everything was made through and for Jesus, the angels would have been his to command, because, as the unique Son of God, he is naturally superior to them. In the book of

Revelation, the angels ceaselessly worship him, the Lamb of God, before the throne of heaven (7:11–17).

Jesus' relationship with the angelic host is also described in Hebrews 1. He is indeed superior to all angels, because it was through him that God created all things: 'For to which of the angels did God ever say, "You are my Son; today I have begotten you?"' (Hebrews v. 5). There is a clear distinction spelled out here between the angels, equipped with winds and flames of fire and called to worship God, and Jesus, the divine pre-existent Son, whose throne is for ever and ever and who has been anointed with the everlasting oil of gladness. This beautiful passage goes on to ask the rhetorical question, 'Are not all angels spirits in the divine service, sent to serve for the sake of those who are to inherit salvation?' (v. 14).

The gift of salvation, won for us by Jesus on the cross, is freely available to all who will open their hearts and lives to him, for, as Luke reminds us, 'Indeed they cannot die any more, because they are like angels and are children of God, being children of the resurrection' (Luke 20:36).

Stephen, the first Christian martyr, should certainly be described in this way. Stephen was one of seven Greek-speaking, or 'Hellenistic', disciples of Jesus who were chosen to assist the apostles in the distribution of gifts to widows, and who became known as the first deacons of the emerging Christian church in Jerusalem. In Acts 6, we read the account of Stephen's short but wonderful ministry, a ministry full of the grace and power that came from the Holy Spirit. Arrested and slandered by malicious false witnesses, he was brought before the Jewish council: 'And all who sat in the council looked intently at him, and they saw that his face was like the face of an angel' (v. 15). In spite of the almost certain knowledge that he was about to die, Stephen must have looked calm and beautiful, his face transfixed with wonder and worship.

He fearlessly addressed the council, giving the history of the Jewish people and ending with words of condemnation, which he must have known could be neither tolerated nor forgiven. He accused them of opposing the Holy Spirit, persecuting God's prophets and being the betrayers and murderers of Jesus.

The enraged priests and scribes ground their teeth at Stephen, but, filled with God's Holy Spirit, he was able to gaze into heaven, where he could see the glory of God, and Jesus standing at his right hand. God's ministering angels must have been all around Stephen as well as being part of the vision, for he was able to pray, even as he was being cruelly stoned to death, 'Lord, do not hold this sin against them' (7:60). These words are like an echo of the words that Stephen's master Jesus cried from the cross: 'Father, forgive them; for they do not know what they are doing' (Luke 23:34).

The role of ministering angels in the scriptures can be seen as a challenge to us to offer food and water to those in need—even those far away who suffer as a result of drought, war or famine, to whose poignant news pictures we can so easily become desensitized. Members of the caring professions, notably nurses, used to be called 'angels', and they are blessed in having the vocation to minister to others in their daily lives. This is also true of doctors, ambulance drivers and paramedics. While the angels ministered directly to Jesus in the wilderness, we can show how much we love him by the way we care for others. 'Truly I tell you, just as you did it to one of the least of these who are members of my family, you did it to me' (Matthew 25:40). If we serve others as if they were Jesus, we are obedient to God by humbling ourselves as he did—and we also open ourselves up to the possibility of worshipping as Stephen did, making angels of us, too.

—— *10* ——

MINISTERING ANGELS:
PERSONAL EXPERIENCES

'Many years ago, when I was four,' Betty told me, 'I had to go into Birmingham Children's Hospital to have my tonsils out. It was the first time I'd ever been away from home and I was very frightened and unhappy. I was put in a cot to sleep, and I didn't like the food— mince, and horrible, slimy, boiled cod.

'After the operation, I just felt wretched. The nurses were kind enough, but busy. I got told off for knocking my water jug over, and family visiting times were limited and strictly adhered to. It's no exaggeration to say that my little heart felt broken! The only thing that made any of it bearable was the small, silver-haired lady who would come in the night when everyone else was asleep, and speak so softly and gently to me as she soothed my brow.

'I mentioned her to my mother, and she spoke to the staff, wanting to thank the woman, who she thought must have been the senior night nurse, for her loving care. But the staff were really surprised, and said so. There was no such nurse in the whole of the hospital!'

Helen recounts a similar visitation while recovering from a hip replacement operation. 'I remember waking up in the middle of the night, just as the door opened and a young male nurse came in. He had a white jacket, black trousers and dark hair.

'"My name is Philip," he told me. "You're very hot. Shall I open a window?"

'He opened the window wide, and I felt more comfortable, and went back to sleep. When I mentioned him to the sister the next day, she was adamant that there was no one called Philip on the staff—in fact, no male nurse at all in that particular section.'

These two experiences bear a striking resemblance to one described in Victor Pearce's book *Miracles and Angels*, under the heading 'The unknown doctor'. A woman who had been gravely ill with depression was visited by a blond-haired doctor who spent an hour at her hospital bedside, speaking encouraging and healing words. The encounter was so special that by the time he left, the patient knew that she had turned the corner and was on the long road to recovery, but when she described the doctor to the ward sister, she had no idea who he was. 'Blond hair! Well, he wouldn't be a member of our doctors' team for this ward—neither of them have blond hair—but I will ask around.' She did, but could trace nobody. She searched the registry, but found absolutely no clue. So who could it have been?[6]

Another strange night-time visitation is recalled by Maria, a member of one of our local church congregations.

'I was going through a very bad patch in my life, and one night, while I was in bed with my small daughter, I had an horrific dream, which woke me up shaking. I said, out loud, "Lord Jesus, please help me!" And a great big wing, full of white feathers, came suddenly over me like the softest duvet! I know I didn't imagine it.

'In a second, all my terrors had gone. I was full of joy, and I laughed. The last thing I remember before falling into the best sleep I'd had for ages was pulling my daughter under the wing with me. During this time in my life, I also kept on finding tiny white feathers—in my handbag, for instance, or between the pages of books. I didn't tell anyone in case they thought I was crazy, but now I really think they were a sign that the angels really were taking care of me!'

The appearance of white feathers is a strange phenomenon, which has been mentioned to me by others who have shared their angelic experiences. Like Maria, these people have come to see them as comfortingly tangible evidence that they are being looked after by someone who may be unseen but who is certainly not far away.

Even without feathers, ministering angels always change lives for the better. A woman whom I will call Mary wrote to me:

'My life was a nightmare; my husband, a very busy GP, was suffering from stress and had been convinced for five years that he had various life-threatening diseases. We spent much of our time trailing from one specialist to another, all of whom could find nothing wrong with him. The rest of the time, he was preoccupied and uninterested in life with me and the children.

'Eventually, I ran out of patience, and one evening, when he decided to admit himself to hospital with heart problems, I let him go alone and I went to bed. I was very upset. I said my prayers as usual and tried to sleep, still holding on to my prayer book.

'I slept fitfully and woke as dawn was breaking and the birds were beginning to sing. I felt the familiar feeling of dread and panic as I remembered the situation I was in, and I rolled over in bed, away from the door, still holding the book. I heard soft footsteps on the bedroom carpet, coming towards me, but for some reason I could not or would not turn over and look. I then felt my hair being gently stroked. I was suddenly overwhelmed by a wonderful feeling of calm and a certain knowledge that everything would be all right. I went back to sleep and slept soundly.

'Later that day, I asked both children separately if they had come to me during the night, but neither of them had left their beds. I am convinced that it was an angel coming to me when I was in most need. Shortly after this, my husband's health returned to normal.'

Ministering angels seem to appear often in the lives of children, especially when they are ill. Paul, now in his late 20s, tells how his parents took him and his elder brother on holiday to Portugal when he was seven years old. He had been feeling off colour, and in the hotel lounge on the day of their arrival, a woman came up to his mother and said, 'Your little boy is very poorly. Let me take him to my husband.'

Paul's parents followed the stranger. Her husband, a tall, grey-haired man, looked at the little boy and said that he was on the brink of pneumonia. He opened his briefcase and gave them some antibiotics. He also said that Paul would feel well enough to be in the swimming-pool by the next day.

At the time, Paul's father was worried because he had just lost his job. He found himself telling the paediatrician, who assured him that he would find a new job when they got home. This all came true. Paul says the whole thing had a surreal quality that he can remember to this day. He doesn't think the couple were 'angels' in the conventional sense, but there was something very strange going on!

Another story, from even further in the past, comes from Doris, a lady who attends our local Methodist church. 'When I was young, we lived in a little old house in Willenhall,' she recounts. 'My little brother, who was 18 months old, contracted double pneumonia. The doctor told my mum he couldn't do anything else for him.

'Next door to us lived a woman my mother wasn't too keen on. She swore and smoked heavily and was pretty scruffy to look at. After the doctor left, this woman came in and asked if she could see my brother. Mum let her go upstairs, and a few minutes later she came clomping back down. "It's all right," she said, in her rough way. "He ain't going to die. There was a big angel over the bed up there. And the angel was shaking its head!"

'My brother did get over his illness,' Doris finishes. 'In fact, he grew up to be a man and we very often told him how an angel had looked after him.'

Stories like this one are passed down in families and communities, and rightly so. Angels are in the lullabies we still sing to our children and grandchildren, and for many people there is something infinitely comforting in the notion that, in the words of a very old song, 'angels are above you, peeping at you, dearie, from the skies'.

There are also the stories that I call 'tales which go around the world', in which we hear of strangers saving people from certain drowning and then disappearing into thin air, or where cars and ambulances are miraculously lifted from the crushed bodies of casualties. Such a story was told to me by Alan, a member of the congregation of St Aiden's church, Leamore, who once saw what he called a 'miracle' when an ambulance rolled down an embankment off the motorway.

'There was absolute chaos as the driver was airlifted to hospital and the passengers moved clear of the wreckage,' he says. 'Then somebody said, "Where's the nurse?" and the people realized there had been somebody else on board, who had completely disappeared! They thought she couldn't possibly have survived, then someone heard the sound of banging from *underneath* the ambulance. The nurse had been thrown straight out, and somehow been pulled under the wheels without being hurt, and there was a pocket of air and a space there that meant she wasn't even scratched!'

A clergy colleague intoduced me to Kate, a woman in her congregation who had experienced something strange on a group camping trip. In the middle of the first night, a woman in the next tent was taken ill, and it became clear that she was having a miscarriage. 'We phoned for an ambulance,' Kate explains, 'and then we prayed. The campsite was really isolated, down twisting lanes, and it was inky black outside. When the ambulance arrived, one of the attendants smiled and said, "What a good idea, to have those people with torches leading the way down the lane. We'd probably never have found you without them!" We all just looked at one another. We hadn't stationed anyone down the lane, but it was obvious that someone had been there!'

There is also an anecdote that appears in several books, in which a man called Geoff goes into a bookshop and meets a Native American man—a stranger who seems to have read every book Geoff is thinking of buying. After some conversation, they decide to go for a beer, and the Native American asks him some challenging questions about his life and lack of faith.

Geoff drops his money on the floor under the table where they are sitting, and when he straightens up from retrieving it, his companion has gone. He asks the barman if he saw him leave, and the barman, perplexed, scratches his head. 'You came in on your own, mate!' he says. 'I thought it was a bit strange when you ordered two pints.'

That night, as he tries to work out what was happening to him, Geoff hears, for the very first time in his life, the voice of God, saying, 'I know you as Geoffrey' (Geoff's baptismal name). Geoff goes to the nearest church, and the vicar is pleased to tell him about Jesus.

I cannot prove the authenticity of this story, but I can prove that God our Father uses ordinary human beings in the role of ministering angels, sometimes in the most unexpected ways and places.

'I'm a retired teacher,' explains Sarah. 'Some years ago, when I had just been through a painful divorce, I was feeling in real spiritual darkness. One afternoon, after all the children had left the classroom, I sat at my school desk and just wept.

'Suddenly I felt someone touch my arm. I turned, and there was a boy from my class standing there. He had dark curls and blue eyes. He was a quiet boy who really looked a bit like an angel. He looked up at me, then, silently, he went to the corner where the sink was. He took a cup and filled it with water.

"Here, Mrs Masters," he said. "Drink this!"

I took the water and drank it, and in that moment, crazy though it might sound, I knew that everything had changed. God was close to me, and I could cope with whatever was going to happen in the future.'

That young boy had felt compelled to stay behind to help his teacher in a small but nevertheless vital way—the way of love, which, by its very simplicity, reminds us of Jesus' commandment to love one another as he has loved us. Jesus himself performed the most lowly of loving acts when he washed his disciples' feet at the last supper. He became a servant as he cared for their most basic needs.

After he had washed their feet, had put on his robe, and had returned to the table, he said to them, 'Do you know what I have done to you? You call

me Teacher and Lord—and you are right, for that is what I am. So if I, your Lord and Teacher, have washed your feet, you also ought to wash one another's feet. For I have set you an example, that you also should do as I have done to you.'
JOHN 13:12–15

There is much evidence that God's ministering angels are still carrying on their Lord's work, whenever our most mundane needs are most miraculously met.

'I ran out of petrol on the motorway,' Margaret told me the other day as I got ready for a church service. 'And while I waited on the hard shoulder, a man drove up in a white van. In the back of it, he had seven or eight cans of petrol. I couldn't believe my eyes! "Oh, I just drive up and down," he smiled, as I began to thank him from the bottom of my heart, "looking for people who've broken down!"'

O God, who hast brought us near to an innumerable company of angels
and to the spirits of just men made perfect;
grant us in our pilgrimage to abide in their fellowship,
and in our heavenly country to become partakers of their joy;
through Jesus Christ our Lord.
WILLIAM BRIGHT (1824–1901)

Bless the Lord, O you his angels,
you mighty ones who do his bidding,
obedient to his spoken word.
PSALM 103:20

Dear Lord, we pray that you will continue to send your ministering angels to all who are sick, or in any kind of need today. We thank you for the special people who act as human angels to others, notably doctors and nurses, but also ambulance drivers, police and fire-fighters. Amen.

11

TRAVELLING COMPANIONS

Now Abraham was old, well advanced in years; and the Lord had blessed Abraham in all things. Abraham said to his servant, the oldest of his house, who had charge of all that he had, 'Put your hand under my thigh and I will make you swear by the Lord, the God of heaven and earth, that you will not get a wife for my son from the daughters of the Canaanites, among whom I live, but will go to my country and to my kindred and get a wife for my son Isaac.' The servant said to him, 'Perhaps the woman may not be willing to follow me to this land; must I then take your son back to the land from which you came?' Abraham said to him, 'See to it that you do not take my son back there. The Lord, the God of heaven, who took me from my father's house and from the land of my birth, and who spoke to me and swore to me, "To your offspring I will give this land", he will send his angel before you; you shall take a wife for my son from there. But if the woman is not willing to follow you, then you will be free from this oath of mine; only you must not take my son back there.' So the servant put his hand under the thigh of Abraham his master and swore to him concerning this matter.

GENESIS 24:1–9

Abraham's senior slave, Eliezer, was sent on an unexpected journey—in search of a bride for his master's son Isaac. Eliezer (whose name in Hebrew means 'help of God') had once been Abraham's heir, as his master had been childless. Ancient documents uncovered near the Tigris river, as well as at other sites, demonstrate that in those times a childless man could adopt one of his own male servants to be heir and guardian of his estate. The words of Genesis 15:2–4 indicate that Abram had either contemplated or already done this:

But Abram said, 'O Lord God, what will you give me, for I continue childless, and the heir of my house is Eliezer of Damascus?' And Abram said, 'You have given me no offspring, and so a slave born in my house is to be my heir.' But the word of the Lord came to him, 'This man shall not be your heir; no one but your very own issue shall be your heir.'

In Abraham's culture, putting a hand under the thigh was the sign of making a binding promise. Following his master's instructions, the faithful servant swore a very solemn oath: he would not find a wife for Isaac from among the loose-living Canaanites, but would bring her back from Abraham's homeland of Mesopotamia.

Eliezer did, however, have a few valid questions. What if the woman he found was unwilling to go with him? Should he then take Isaac back to his father's country? But Abraham was so certain that his instructions were right that he cited God's promise: 'To your offspring I will give this land' (24:7). He promised Eliezer that an angel would go before him on his travels.

Near to the city of his destination, the servant prayed for God's help in his task (vv. 12–14). He asked that the girl he was seeking for his master might identify herself by agreeing to give water not only to him but also to his camels. Even before he had finished speaking, there appeared the beautiful Rebekah, daughter of Bethuel, to whom Abraham was related by marriage. Like other women in the tribe, Rebekah would have visited the well twice daily to draw water for the family. It was also a good place to meet and chat.

On this day, however, Rebekah had a surprise waiting for her. She saw a stranger and responded to his request for water by offering also to draw water for his camels. When Rebekah did exactly as he asked her to do, proving beyond doubt that she was the right girl for Isaac, Eliezer worshipped the Lord, and said, 'Blessed be the Lord, the God of my master Abraham, who has not forsaken his steadfast love and his faithfulness towards my master. As for me, the Lord has led me on the way to the house of my master's kin' (v. 27).

Later, enjoying the hospitality of his hosts, Eliezer retold the story of his journey to Rebekah's father Bethuel and her brother Laban, and joyfully shared the news that Abraham's promise had been fulfilled, and he had not made the journey alone: 'I said to my master, "Perhaps the woman will not follow me." But he said to me, "The Lord, before whom I walk, will send his angel with you and make your way successful. You shall get a wife for my son from my kindred, from my father's house"' (vv. 39–40).

Rebekah's family were convinced that these instructions came from God. The role of the angel was central to this belief, because he had indeed made the journey successful, not only for Eliezer but for his master, God's servant, Abraham.

Travelling-companion angels are present in the Exodus account of Moses leading the people of Israel out of the land of Egypt and across the Red Sea. Freed from Pharaoh, but tired of wandering in the wilderness, the Israelites complained to their ageing human liberator—especially when, on nearing the Red Sea, they saw the Egyptians advancing on them:

They said to Moses, 'Was it because there were no graves in Egypt that you have taken us away to die in the wilderness? What have you done to us, bringing us out of Egypt? Is this not the very thing we told you in Egypt, "Let us alone, and let us serve the Egyptians"? For it would have been better for us to serve the Egyptians than to die in the wilderness.'
EXODUS 14:11–12

Even before he saw the miracle that was about to take place, Moses reassured the disconsolate and terrified people, 'The Lord will fight for you, and you have only to keep still' (v. 14). Moses then listened to the precise instructions God gave him. The Israelites were to go forward, and he was to lift up his staff and stretch out his hand over the sea and divide it, so that the people could walk safely over on dry land. 'The angel of God who was going before the Israelite army moved and went behind them; and the pillar of cloud moved from in front of them and took its place behind them. It came between the army of Egypt and the army of Israel' (vv. 19–20). Ever after, it was widely accepted and celebrated that it was an angel who had brought God's chosen people out of their slavery under Pharaoh: 'And when we cried to the Lord, he heard our voice, and sent an angel and brought us out of Egypt' (Numbers 20:16).

After the parting of the Red Sea, Moses' task was to continue to lead the children of Israel towards the promised land. God reassured him:

I am going to send an angel in front of you, to guard you on the way and to bring you to the place that I have prepared. Be attentive to him and listen to his voice; do not rebel against him, for he will not pardon your transgression; for my name is in him. But if you listen attentively to his voice and do all that I say, then I will be an enemy to your enemies and a foe to your foes.
EXODUS 23:20–22

This travelling-companion angel is also a guardian and a guide, and he promises protection for the future for those who will both listen to him and stay obedient to God.

In the apocryphal book of Tobit, accepted as scripture by some parts of the Church, we read the story of Tobias and the angel, in which the young Tobias, with his dog, unknowingly journeys with the archangel Raphael and finds a cure for his father Tobit's blindness as well as a wife for himself. The family are deeply grateful to the wise and caring stranger who has done so much for them. But when Tobit tries to thank him by giving him half of his entire possessions, Raphael calls both him and Tobias aside and tells them the truth:

'I am Raphael, one of the seven holy angels who present the prayers of the saints and enter into the presence of the Holy One.' They were both alarmed; and they fell upon their faces, for they were afraid. But he said to

them, 'Do not be afraid; you will be safe. But praise God for ever. For I did not come as a favour on my part, but by the will of our God. Therefore praise him for ever. All these days I merely appeared to you and did not eat or drink, but you were seeing a vision. And now give thanks to God, for I am ascending to him who sent me. Write in a book everything that has happened.' Then they stood up; but they saw him no more. So they confessed the great and wonderful works of God, and acknowledged that the angel of the Lord had appeared to them.

TOBIT 12:15–22 (RSV)

An angel of the Lord appeared to the apostle Paul and became his travelling companion on board ship. Paul was chosen by God, against all the odds, to be an apostle of Jesus Christ. Paul's birth name was Saul, and, as the son of a strict Pharisee, he had been brought up according to the Hebrew law. By his own later admission, he persecuted the followers of Jesus, whom he saw as members of a dangerous heretical sect. He was present at the stoning of Stephen and then, not content with cleaning up Jerusalem, he got authority from the high priest to pursue Christians wherever they might be found. It came to his ears that they were stirring up trouble in the synagogues in Damascus, and so he set out for that Syrian city with murder in his heart.

It was on the road to Damascus that the incredible happened. Saul, soon to be for ever known as Paul, met the Lord Jesus Christ in a vision. A light from heaven blinded him and he heard the voice of Jesus telling him to go to the city and wait there for his instructions. 'Saul got up from the ground, and though his eyes were open, he could see nothing; so they led him by the hand and brought him into Damascus. For three days he was without sight, and neither ate nor drank' (Acts 9:8–9).

After spending time in Damascus with Ananias and the other disciples, Paul, with his sight regained, started an amazing new campaign: he began to preach in the synagogues, 'and immediately he began to proclaim Jesus… saying, "He is the Son of God"' (v. 20).

We owe much of our knowledge about the early church to Paul.

He dared all, and sacrificed much in order to fulfil his special ministry, travelling many miles across the known world. If anyone needed an angel as a travelling companion, Paul did! And nowhere was he made more aware of this angel than when he and his companions were caught in a violent storm at sea (Acts 27).

On their way to Rome, they began to sail past Crete, close to the shore. Soon, the north-east wind rushed down and drove the little ship into dangerous waters. So violently were they pounded by the storm that next day they had to throw the cargo overboard, followed by the ship's tackle. The storm raged for many more days, and in complete darkness, abandoned even by the sun and stars, the travellers lost all hope of being saved.

It was then, when they had been without food for a long time, that Paul stood up among them and made his announcement about the protection God had afforded them in the shape of his angel: 'I urge you now to keep up your courage… For last night, there stood by me an angel of the Lord… and he said, "Do not be afraid, Paul; you must stand before the emperor; and indeed, God has granted safety to all those who are sailing with you"' (Acts 27:22–24).

The angel's words came true: Paul and his shipmates survived, and although the book of Acts ends before any specific account of a meeting, the apostle did have to stand before emperors and kings before his amazing ministry on earth came to an end. The heavenly being travelling with him was obviously to be trusted.

Trust is implicit, too, in the story of a very different journey: the journey out of life itself. Jesus tells the parable of the rich man and Lazarus:

There was a rich man who was dressed in purple and fine linen and who feasted sumptuously every day. And at his gate lay a poor man named Lazarus, covered with sores, who longed to satisfy his hunger with what fell from the rich man's table; even the dogs would come and lick his sores. The poor man died and was carried away by the angels to be with Abraham. The rich man also died and was buried.
LUKE 16:19–22

There were no accompanying angels for the rich man. Jesus tells us that he went to Hades, and eternal torment, and although he pleaded with Lazarus, whom he could see in eternal bliss, there was no escaping his deserved punishment for his cruelly self-centred life on earth.

This rich man was, clearly, not one of the men of faith who are described so inspiringly in the wonderful eleventh chapter of Hebrews. The story of God's whole creation, and his subsequent relationship with those with whom he chose to share it, is set out there, from Abel to Abraham, Moses and other Israelite heroes. Many of those whose names appear on this amazing roll call were accompanied in their journeys of faith by angels, who were only too willing to obey God's command and travel with them. Later in Hebrews, we read of a 'cloud of witnesses' surrounding us on our journey. Surely angels are among these witnesses!

Therefore, since we are surrounded by so great a cloud of witnesses, let us also lay aside every weight and the sin that clings so closely, and let us run with perseverance the race that is set before us, looking to Jesus the pioneer and perfecter of our faith, who for the sake of the joy that was set before him endured the cross, disregarding its shame, and has taken his seat at the right hand of the throne of God.
HEBREWS 12:1–2

Angels as travelling companions appear in the scriptures where a specific journey is required that is vital to God's plan. Abraham could not have been the father of nations, with descendants as plentiful as stars or grains of sand, had he not found a wife for his son Isaac; Paul could not have continued his travels, taking the good news of Jesus to the ends of the earth, had he not been accompanied by a presence who stood beside him on the deck of a rolling ship. In the journey of faith, the Bible tells us, we are surrounded by a cloud of witnesses, which must include angels. Although angels are not always specifically mentioned, the final journey, to death, is often described in the Old Testament as being 'gathered to one's people'. According to Jesus, however, it is none other than angels who carry the righteous poor man into the paradise he so richly deserves.

12

TRAVELLING COMPANIONS: PERSONAL EXPERIENCES

In 1996, Andrew had to travel from Hull to Doncaster, and then to London. Although he was 20 and an undergraduate, he had never been that far away from home before, and was feeling nervous. He had been accepted by a mission agency for a short course in Israel, and was travelling to spend a weekend with the other members of the group making the trip. Anxious about everything, he spent the night before his journey in prayer.

On the train from Hull, Andrew noticed an unremarkable-looking woman in her early 40s who seemed to be staring at him very hard. At Doncaster, while he waited for his connection, she came up to him and said, 'You're going to King's Cross, aren't you?' Surprised, Andrew said he was. The woman then suggested that they travel together, and although she was a complete stranger, Andrew found himself agreeing. He no longer felt nervous and began instead to look forward to the journey. It was as if she put him instantly at ease.

On the train, the woman talked about all sorts of things, and he listened. She said nothing that particularly identified her as a Christian, but had a down-to-earth generosity about her. When the drinks trolley came round, she bought him a coffee. 'I know students don't have much money,' she said, although Andrew didn't recall telling her he was a student. When he tried to thank her, she held up her hand, and said, 'You must promise me that sometime in the future, when you're travelling, you will buy another student a drink.'

At King's Cross, the woman took him to the tube station and showed him the map of where he had to go. Then, as if he were a very precious child, she bought him his ticket and put him on the train. On the platform, beforehand, they hugged each other. 'I didn't want to leave,' Andrew confesses, 'but by the time the train doors closed behind me, she had gone. It might sound stupid, but I've always been sure that she was an angel whom God sent to make that journey with me.'

An older man called Ted, who attends one of our local Methodist churches, tells the dramatic story of how he travelled with an angel in his car, and the angel took over the wheel and saved his life.

'I was heading towards the motorway,' Ted recounts, 'but suddenly, the steering wheel just wouldn't let me take the car in that direction! I tried and tried, but it really felt as if someone else had taken the wheel out of my hand. All I could do was to let the car go the way that this unseen power seemed to want to take it.

'I had no alternative but to avoid that motorway junction and get on at the next. It was then that I heard that there had been a fatal pile-up minutes before, on the stretch I had planned to take. I don't know if it was an angel, but there was certainly somebody travelling with me that day!'

A visible angelic travelling companion was seen by Emmie, a lady from my own parish.

'When I was eight, I was taking a short cut home from church across the graveyard. It was dark and I was really scared. I said, out loud, "Oh God! I wish I was home!" Suddenly, I realized that there was a tall man at my side. He looked down at me really kindly and said, "Don't worry, my dear. Jesus is looking after you." Then he just disappeared. I still pass the place where it happened, and I always remember it!'

Worries about travelling to visit a relative were causing Edna sleepless nights and bad dreams. 'It was not long after my husband's death,' she told me, 'and the first time I would be going any distance without him. One night, when I was very het up, I dreamt that my husband came back and drove me to my destination in our old car. That didn't seem so strange until the next day, when my daughter-in-law, the present owner of the car, visited me. She said, "Oh, Edna! I had such a peculiar dream last night. I dreamt the car had been stolen!"

'I'm certain that the dreams were messages from God, telling me not to worry—that someone would be with me on the journey, and prompting my daughter-in-law to offer to drive me!'

In his book *Miracles and Angels*, Victor Pearce talks about being accompanied by angels on a missionary journey across Bombay. He had been waiting at the wrong airport when one, and then another, came unexpectedly to his aid:

My ticket was in a closed folder in my hand and no labels displayed my route, so I was greatly surprised when, out of the corner of my eye, I saw an officer begin to walk rapidly my way.

She reached me and said urgently: 'You are at the wrong airport! You should be at the Jet Indian Airport, not here. Come quickly! Hurry or you'll miss your plane!'

She took hold of my hand and pulled me towards a youth with a trolley. I hadn't noticed him before. He took my baggage and put it on the trolley. 'Hurry! Hurry! This youngster will show you the way.'

He did just that, but when I offered him a tip, he just shook his head. I just managed to catch the plane, and when I'd settled into my seat, I began to think about the incident. There were one or two strange things about it. First, how had the uniformed lady known I was at the wrong airport? She couldn't see my ticket. And how had she known I was English? Thirdly, that's the first porter I've known to refuse a tip. Had I been rescued by an angel in uniform, and an angel youth? Had I not been rescued and put on the right plane, I would have missed the meetings attended by 45,000 people, to whom I brought the Good News of Jesus Christ.[7]

It is not always necessary to be a churchgoer in order to be aware of the phenomenon of angels coming to 'fetch' people at the point of their death. My own great-grandmother, on her deathbed at the age of 92, reported that her late husband was 'up the corner' and waiting for her. She had never expressed anything more than nominal Christian faith.

Ministering to the bereaved through funerals and memorial services, I have encountered many people who, though never likely to become regular churchgoers, still believe in the travelling-companion angels who take their loved ones over the border into a new life. One dear old lady in Pensnett stays in my memory because she spent her last few days rapturously talking to the angels around her bed. In spite of the circumstances, it was a joy to go and visit Gladys in hospital because we knew that, like John the Divine, she was being given a preview of what lay beyond that heavenly door.

Nurses and long-time carers report similar experiences. June, a nurse who goes to the Willenhall Christian Fellowship, talks about the day her own mother died: 'There was a presence in the room, a strange light. Both me and my sister saw it, and we believe it was the angel who came to take Mum home.'

Another friend, Joyce, says, 'My mother told me about something that happened when she was a little girl. She was very close to another girl, Flora, who was ill with tuberculosis. The night Flora died, my mother felt called to look through the front window. She looked out and saw Flora standing there in her Sunday dress and a pretty picture hat she'd never seen before. She had another little girl with her, and looked very happy.' Flora waved her hand to Joyce's mother, who went to fetch her own mother, but the little girl had disappeared. Next morning, they found out that she had died in the night.

Another, more recent experience deals with the death of a husband. Kath, now in her 80s, remembers, 'My husband was only in his 40s when he was diagnosed with kidney failure. It was in the days before dialysis and transplants, and I was told, very brutally, by a hospital doctor that he wasn't going to recover. I was really angry with God that he had allowed this illness—our two children were still very young. I went to my sister's, in fact, after receiving the news, and said, "There is no God!"

'I hated the thought of my lovely young husband having to die, and I devoted myself to nursing him at home. Only later did I realize where I was getting the strength from, and it came about because, the day he died, my husband suddenly called me and said, really excitedly, "Look who's here, Kath! It's my uncle Albert! He's come for me!"

'His favourite uncle had been dead for many years, so I knew he couldn't really be in the room. But my husband could see him, and was content. Within the hour, my husband had gone. His suffering was over and he was at peace—a peace that I felt echoed in my own heart, in spite of the years of grief and loneliness that I still knew lay ahead.'

Billy Graham says, 'When my time to die comes, an angel will be there to comfort me. He will give me peace and joy even at that most critical hour, and usher me into the presence of God, and I will dwell with the Lord for ever.'[8] These experiences of angels travelling to earth to be with us on our most critical and potentially frightening journeys make me think of the words of that old but still popular hymn 'Blessed assurance', written by the blind American composer Francis Jane van Alstyne, better known as Fanny Crosby (1820–1915).

Angels descending bring from above
Echoes of mercy, whispers of love.

Come to meet him, angels of the Lord,
welcome his soul, present him to God the most high.
THE CATHOLIC FUNERAL SERVICE

There is no place where God is not,
Wherever I go, there God is.
Now and always he upholds me with his power
And keeps me safe in his love.
AUTHOR UNKNOWN

O God, who hast brought us near to an innumerable company of angels and to the spirits of just men made perfect; grant us in our pilgrimage to abide in their fellowship, and in our heavenly country to become partakers of their joy; through Jesus Christ our Lord.

WILLIAM BRIGHT (1824–1901)

Heavenly Father, we need dread no journey on this earth, knowing that your envoy travels with us. Thank you for the evidence that your holy angels stay near those who must commute long distances each day, or travel to other countries by air or sea. We pray especially for all whose earthly journey is done, that the angels will bear them safely to your heavenly kingdom, where they will see you face to face. Amen.

---– *13* ---–

ANGELS IN WORSHIP

In the year that King Uzziah died, I saw the Lord sitting on a throne, high and lofty; and the hem of his robe filled the temple. Seraphs were in attendance above him; each had six wings: with two they covered their faces, and with two they covered their feet, and with two they flew. And one called to another and said: 'Holy, holy, holy is the Lord of hosts; the whole earth is full of his glory.'
ISAIAH 6:1–3

This Old Testament passage is often used for ordination services, and no wonder, for the imagery is very powerful. It is full of worship in the true sense of that word, as the seraphs give God his 'worth' and the scene is set for Isaiah's dramatic call into the Lord's service.

The Sanctus, which is Latin for 'holy', is an ancient hymn. It is still said or sung as part of many Holy Communion services:

> *Therefore with angels and archangels,*
> *and with all the company of heaven,*
> *we proclaim your great and glorious name,*
> *for ever praising you and saying:*
> *'Holy, holy, holy Lord,*
> *God of power and might,*
> *heaven and earth are full of your glory,*
> *Hosanna in the highest.'* [9]

'Hosanna', meaning, in Hebrew, 'O save', is an exclamation of adoration. Throughout the scriptures, we find many examples of the angels praising and adoring God.

The joyful message that the shepherds in the fields around

Bethlehem heard on Christmas Eve over two millennia ago still best expresses angelic worship, and it is significant that we human beings are so enthusiastically invited to join in: 'And suddenly there was with the angel a multitude of the heavenly host, praising God and saying, "Glory to God in the highest heaven, and on earth peace among those whom he favours!"' (Luke 2:13–14).

Like the Sanctus, the Gloria has been incorporated into formal worship and is a beautiful part of the traditional liturgy used Sunday by Sunday in churches throughout the world:

> *Glory to God in the highest,*
> *and peace to his people on earth.*
> *Lord God, heavenly King,*
> *almighty God and Father,*
> *we worship you, we give you thanks,*
> *we praise you for your glory.*
> *Lord Jesus Christ, only Son of the Father,*
> *Lord God, Lamb of God,*
> *you take away the sin of the world;*
> *have mercy on us;*
> *you are seated at the right hand of the Father:*
> *receive our prayer.*
> *For you alone are the Holy One,*
> *you alone are the Lord,*
> *you alone are the Most High, Jesus Christ,*
> *with the Holy Spirit,*
> *in the glory of God the Father.*
> *Amen.*[10]

The Gloria has at its heart the worship of Jesus Christ, and in the letter of Paul to the Colossians, the reason is made very clear: 'He is the image of the invisible God, the firstborn of all creation; for in him all things in heaven and on earth were created, things visible and invisible, whether thrones or dominions or rulers or powers— all things have been created through him and for him' (Colossians 1:15–16).

Jesus is superior to all other beings, and nowhere is the worth and glory of Jesus more evident than in the book of Revelation. Here we find descriptions of perpetual worship in heaven. In chapter 4, a door is opened so that John, the recorder of the strange and wonderful visions shown to him by an angel, can actually see all that is taking place. There are echoes here of the Sanctus that Isaiah heard, and which reverberates down the centuries. John's image of heavenly worship has been inspiring writers, artists and composers ever since it was written in the first century AD. At that time, the church was facing persecution so violent that it seemed unlikely to survive. John was imprisoned for his faith on the island of Patmos, having spent his life working for the survival of the seven churches of the mainland, of which the chief was Ephesus.

John begins his book by describing how he received his revelation from God, through an angel. He then records specific messages from Jesus to the seven churches in Asia Minor. Despite its sometimes uncomfortably graphic imagery, the worship of Jesus continues to be paramount throughout. Revelation is, in fact, a celebration of the words of the writer of Hebrews: 'For to which of the angels did God ever say, "You are my Son; today I have begotten you"? Or again, "I will be his Father, and he will be my Son"? And again, when he brings the firstborn into the world, he says, "Let all God's angels worship him"' (Hebrews 1:5–6).

The conventional image that most of us have in mind is of angels worshipping around God's heavenly throne. Certainly many hymns have been inspired by this theme, from 'Ye holy angels bright' to 'Angels from the realms of glory' and 'Angel voices'. It is an image that has captivated authors as well as famous artists down the centuries. An anonymous third-century hymn says:

> *May all the angels in the heavens sing:*
> *'Amen! Amen! Amen!*
> *Power, praise, honour, eternal glory to God,*
> *the only giver of grace.*
> *Amen! Amen! Amen!'*

The Victorian sage Thomas Carlyle wrote, 'Music is well said to be the speech of angels.' Much later, Billy Graham asserts that angels have a superior capacity to offer praise because they are close to God, and have been serenading him with their music from time immemorial: 'I believe angel choirs will sing in eternity to the glory of God and the supreme delight of the redeemed. I think most earthly music will seem to us to have been in the "minor key" in comparison to what we are going to hear in heaven.'[11]

To hear the angels singing here on earth is an amazing experience, and one that I have actually known. When I was ten years old, my great-grandmother died. My younger brother and I shared a room, and I was very much aware that it was next door to where Granny Coley had been 'laid out'. The memory of the night before the funeral is still very vivid, and many years later I included it in one of my books:

It's as the thought and the prayer fuse together that the angel voices come. Far away and yet near, wafting in on the air of that clear night. I catch my breath and dig my fingers into my sleeping brother's arm. But only I can hear the singing. At least, that's what I think until the next morning. When I get up and go downstairs, I hear my mother telling the next-door aunt: 'I know Gran's all right. Last night, I heard the angels singing.'[12]

Sue Hughes, a member of St Stephen's church, Willenhall, and a friend I have made through the writing of this book, tells me that such experiences are by no means uncommon. 'I have heard the angels singing many, many times after someone has died,' she says. 'To accept that they are very near to them, and to us, is a wonderful, comforting thing, and I believe they give us courage as well as energy through their worship of God.'

Another friend, who is a priest, describes her experience of singing with the angels when she was deeply in prayer one day. 'I was a long way from home, and had been feeling very vulnerable,' says Sandy. 'Finding myself actually there, worshipping God with his angels, just made me want to go to heaven as soon as possible!'

Hope Price describes many experiences of angels singing, including a phenomenon that took place at the Yorkshire Showground in the early 1980s, when thousands of Christians had gathered for the Dales Bible Week, an opportunity for teaching, worship and relaxation. On several nights, at about midnight, the police were called by local residents complaining about the volume of singing coming from the showground. On investigating, they found the whole camp absolutely quiet, with most people in their tents, and the music pavilion deserted and in darkness.

Other local residents, however, enjoyed the 'most beautiful music' and called at the gates during the day to enquire who had been singing so exquisitely. The Christian campers heard the wondrous choir as well... Humans weren't singing but the angels were, and the sound we heard could not have been made by human voices, however good they were.[13]

For many of the people I have interviewed, the church has been the setting for their angelic sighting or encounter. It could be a movement caught for ever in the turning of a head or the blinking of an eye. It could be the knowledge that there are beings joyfully giving praise to God when someone, acknowledging that they are a sinner, goes up to the altar and repents. And that praise is reverberating all the way from God's throne in heaven. The church is also very often the setting for that wonderful experience we call 'the communion of saints', when, strange though it may sound, a body of worshippers knows that those who have gone before them are somehow joining in, with an enthusiasm we have not yet known, in the endless praise of our God.

The Bible tells us that angels worship around God's throne, giving honour to Jesus. At special moments, chosen by God alone, we humans seem also tuned in to hear their celestial music.

ANGELS IN JUDGMENT

As I looked, a stormy wind came out of the north: a great cloud with brightness around it and fire flashing forth continually, and in the middle of the fire, something like gleaming amber. In the middle of it was something like four living creatures. This was their appearance: they were of human form. Each had four faces, and each of them had four wings... Over the heads of the living creatures there was something like a dome, shining like crystal, spread out above their heads. Under the dome their wings were stretched out straight, one towards another; and each of the creatures had two wings covering its body... And above the dome over their heads there was something like a throne, in appearance like sapphire; and seated above the likeness of a throne was something that seemed like a human form. Upwards from what appeared like the loins I saw something like gleaming amber, something that looked like fire enclosed all round; and downwards from what looked like the loins I saw something that looked like fire, and there was a splendour all round. Like the bow in a cloud on a rainy day, such was the appearance of the splendour all round. This was the appearance of the likeness of the glory of the Lord.

EZEKIEL 1:4–6, 22–23, 26–28

The Old Testament book of Ezekiel begins with a vision in which, like Isaiah, a prophet received his call from God. A Hebrew priest and prophet of the exile, Ezekiel saw four living creatures in human form, in a kind of gleaming amber chariot (vv. 5–6). The living creatures, called 'cherubim' in Ezekiel 10, are described as having four faces: a human face, as well as the faces of a lion, a cherub and an eagle. They came suddenly, out of a stormy wind, and 'the living creatures darted to and fro, like a flash of lightning' (v. 14).

Many of Ezekiel's visions were about judgment. He was sent by God to the people of Israel and was forewarned that they would not listen to him, that they would have 'a hard forehead and a stubborn heart' (3:7). He fulfilled his mission by pouring out his soul in condemnation of the people of God for their failure to be worthy of that name, and proclaimed the disaster of the fall of Jerusalem as the deserved punishment of God. Ezekiel was called upon, in another vision, to eat a scroll described as having writing on the front and on the back. Normally, ancient scrolls were written on one side only, so the implication here is that the scroll was thoroughly saturated with words of divine judgment: 'words of lamentation and mourning and woe' (2:10).

There are parallels between the books of Ezekiel and Revelation, one being that on the island of Patmos, John was also asked to eat a scroll. But his instruction was delivered by an angel:

And I saw another mighty angel coming down from heaven, wrapped in a cloud, with a rainbow above his head; his face was like the sun, and his legs were like pillars of fire. He held a little scroll open in his hand. Setting his right foot on the sea and his left foot on the land, he gave a great shout, like a lion roaring. And when he shouted, the seven thunders sounded... Then the voice that I had heard from heaven spoke to me again, saying, 'Go, take the scroll that is open in the hand of the angel who is standing on the sea and on the land.' So I went to the angel and told him to give me the little scroll; and he said to me, 'Take it, and eat; it will be bitter to your stomach, but sweet as honey in your mouth.' So I took the little scroll from the hand of the angel and ate it; it was sweet as honey in my mouth, but when I had eaten it, my stomach was made bitter. Then they said to me, 'You must prophesy again about many peoples and nations and languages and kings.'

REVELATION 10:1–3, 8–11

The book of Revelation can be said to reveal the true and full identity of Jesus and his message of eternal life. John proclaims that Jesus will surely return to vindicate the righteous but also to judge the wicked. To each of the seven churches that are his intended readers, John sends a message from Jesus—and the message is given through the angel who has charge of each church. For each church, there is a word of encouragement, reproach or condemnation. Jesus calls them, through their angels, to live in righteousness as they wait for the panoramic drama, portrayed so vividly in Revelation, to begin to unfold. This drama incorporates plagues, lakes of fire and seven avenging angels whom God commands to pour out the seven bowls of the wrath of God:

The seventh angel poured his bowl into the air, and a loud voice came out of the temple, from the throne, saying, 'It is done!' And there came flashes of lightning, rumblings, peals of thunder, and a violent earthquake, such as had not occurred since people were upon the earth, so violent was that earthquake. The great city was split into three parts, and the cities of the nations fell.

REVELATION 16:17–19

There are many other places in the Bible where God is said to have used his angels to carry out his judgments. In Latin, the word translated 'host', which we associate with angels, can mean 'an army', and, as illustrated by Elisha's experience in 2 Kings 6, the Lord of hosts is more than capable of sending his soldier angels.

In Genesis 18, angels play a part in the judgment on Sodom and Gomorrah. There we read how God sent angels to warn Abraham that these two wicked cities were to be destroyed. Abraham's nephew Lot and his family lived in Sodom, and Abraham pleaded with God to spare the city, almost bargaining with him about the number of righteous people within it. Two angels, who appeared as ordinary men, then visited Sodom to warn Lot and his family, and were in danger of being assaulted by Sodom's inhabitants, who found them physically attractive (19:1–6). Lot and his family subsequently escaped the destruction of the city, although Lot's wife looked back and was turned into a pillar of salt (v. 26).

A fierce angel was also sent to punish Israel after King David angered the Lord by his method of taking a military census— perhaps for the mistaken motive of self-glory rather than God's honour. The Lord's anger, however, does seem to have quickly abated:

So the Lord sent a pestilence on Israel from that morning until the appointed time; and seventy thousand of the people died, from Dan to Beer-sheba. But when the angel stretched out his hand toward Jerusalem to destroy it, the Lord relented concerning the evil, and said to the angel who was bringing destruction among the people, 'It is enough; now stay your hand.' The angel of the Lord was then by the threshing-floor of Araunah the Jebusite. When David saw the angel who was destroying the people, he said to the Lord, 'I alone have sinned, and I alone have done wickedly; but these sheep, what have they done? Let your hand, I pray, be against me and against my father's house.'
2 SAMUEL 24:15–17

In 2 Kings 19, we read how King Hezekiah received a letter from the commander of the warring Assyrian forces. Hezekiah asked for God's help, and God gave the answer to the prophet Isaiah: not one Assyrian arrow would be fired into the city. For David's sake, God would give Jerusalem his utmost protection. That very night, the Assyrian camp was struck by just one angel, and 185,000 soldiers were found dead on the battlefield next day (v. 35).

One of the best-known incidents involving angels carrying out God's judgment must surely be the destruction of the firstborn of the Egyptians, when the people of Israel were still living as slaves in Egypt. The Lord commanded Moses and Aaron that on the fourteenth day of a certain month, at dusk, each Israelite family should slaughter a lamb or kid, daub its blood on their lintel and doorposts, and roast its flesh for a sacrificial meal.

This is how you shall eat it: your loins girded, your sandals on your feet, and your staff in your hand; and you shall eat it hurriedly. It is the passover of the Lord. For I will pass through the land of Egypt that night, and I will strike down every firstborn in the land of Egypt, both human beings and animals; on all the gods of Egypt I will execute judgments: I am the Lord. The blood shall be a sign for you on the houses where you live; when I see the blood, I will pass over you, and no plague shall destroy you when I strike the land of Egypt.

EXODUS 12:11–13

The destroying angel, whom we also read about in the New Testament letters of 1 Corinthians (10:10) and Hebrews (11:28), was, to the Egyptians, an agent of death and judgment, as well as being God's liberator for the people of Israel. This is clear evidence that angels should not always be seen as consoling!

The Bible demonstrates very often that God's ways are not our ways, and nowhere is this more apparent than in the quirky little story about Balaam's donkey and the angel who was acting in the capacity of an overseer and a judge. Balaam, a Mesopotamian soothsayer, is believed to have lived in the 13th century BC, in Pethor (in present-day Iraq). Balak, the king of Moab, sent dignitaries to him with a large reward, requesting his spiritual aid against the people of Israel, who had pitched their tents in the plains of Moab on their way to the promised land: 'Come now, curse this people for me, since they are stronger than I; perhaps I shall be able to defeat them and drive them from the land; for I know that whomsoever you bless is blessed, and whomsoever you curse is cursed' (Numbers 22:6).

Balaam asked for God's help in this task and even though he was a foreigner and a soothsayer, God spoke to him. At first, the Lord said to Balaam, 'You shall not go with them; you shall not curse the people, for they are blessed' (v. 12). But then, another delegation arrived from Balak, so the Lord let Balaam go. As he was making his way through a vineyard on his donkey, the animal suddenly refused to go on, and Balaam lost his temper. What Balaam did not know was that the donkey's path was being blocked by an angel with a drawn sword (an echo of the sword-wielding angel whom God appointed to guard Eden after the expulsion of Adam and Eve in Genesis 3).

When the donkey, understandably, turned off the road and went into a field, Balaam struck it to make it turn back. The angel of the Lord then appeared on a narrow path, hemmed in by walls, and so the donkey scraped against the wall, also scraping its master's foot. Balaam struck it again. When the angel moved yet again, completely blocking the donkey's path, the animal's response was to lie down under Balaam, who, furious by now, hit it with his stick. It was then that a miracle happened, although it is described in a very understated way:

Then the Lord opened the mouth of the donkey, and it said to Balaam, 'What have I done to you, that you have struck me these three times?' Balaam said to the donkey, 'Because you have made a fool of me! I wish I had a sword in my hand! I would kill you right now!' But the donkey said to Balaam, 'Am I not your donkey, which you have ridden all your life to this day? Have I been in the habit of treating you this way?' And he said, 'No.'

NUMBERS 22:28–30

Balaam's eyes were then opened by God, so that he too saw the angel of the Lord with his mighty sword in his hand. Balaam, while strangely undisturbed by a talking donkey, was thoroughly overcome, falling on his face before the angel, who proceeded to give him the chastisement he deserved: 'The angel of the Lord said to him, "Why have you struck your donkey these three times? I have come out as an adversary, because your way is perverse before me"' (v. 32).

Balaam was contrite, admitting that he had sinned and offering to go home. The angel instructed him to go with the men who were approaching, but to say only the words that the angel gave him. The king of Moab and his courtiers came out to meet Balaam to take him to the Israelite encampment. There, to the king's fury, Balaam began to bless the Israelites instead of cursing them. The spirit of God had come upon him and he prophesied that 'a star shall come out of Jacob, and a sceptre shall rise out of Israel; it shall crush the borderlands of Moab' (24:17).

Despite his past life, Balaam had learnt from his angelic encounter. It brought him closer to God and made him a more obedient servant, someone who, at least for a time, could unconsciously emulate the trust and faithfulness of his humble donkey.

This attitude of the serving heart is what Jesus calls us all to exhibit when he comes again in judgment and glory:

When the Son of Man comes in his glory, and all the angels with him, then he will sit on the throne of his glory. All the nations will be gathered before him, and he will separate people one from another as a shepherd separates the sheep from the goats, and he will put the sheep at his right hand and the goats at the left.
MATTHEW 25:31–33

Those whom Jesus places at his right hand will be those who have fed him and given him water, welcomed him as a stranger, clothed him when naked, taken care of him when he was sick, and visited him in prison. Asked by the puzzled righteous ones when all this happened, he replies, 'Truly I tell you, just as you did it to one of the least of these who are members of my family, you did it to me' (v. 40). The passage goes on to describe graphically how those who do not fulfil these obligations of love towards the least of Jesus' worldwide human family are despatched to the eternal fire that awaits the devil and his angels. Like that of the selfish rich man, their punishment will be eternal and non-negotiable.

The poet Henry Wadsworth Longfellow once described how, after death, we each encounter two angels who record all our earthly deeds in great books. The one who writes down the good deeds flies straight up to heaven with it, while the other keeps his book open, hoping against hope that we will repent before it is too late.

This may seem a typically Victorian idea, yet the image of angels in judgment persists even in the contemporary literature of magazine stories and meditation scripts intended for use in modern-day worship. A short story by Elizabeth Ann Peters, published in *Woman Alive* in July 2004, begins, 'I'm standing at the end of the pier, about to jump off, when in flies an angel with a big red book in his hands.' The angel tells the story of the narrator's life. In fact, the title of the story is 'This Is Your Life'. Before she knows what is happening, the narrator is whisked away into the clouds to face a whole host of angelic beings, all supposedly from her past. As her life passes before her, she is brought face to face with the dark spectres of Rejection, Isolation, Independence and Shame.

The final figure she meets is Jesus, who brings with him six more angels. These are the invisible friends by whom she has been surrounded ever since she let him into her life. They are Love, Security, Belonging, Peace, Joy and Acceptance.

In his book *He Was In the World*, John Bell of the Iona Community includes a meditation called 'On the Bus', about an encounter on a bus between a passenger and a mysterious old woman: 'The bus waits, then on comes an old woman, not very tall, but quite stout, wearing an old brown coat, and a cheap green headsquare… And under her arm she carries a bundle of newspapers… evening newspapers.'

The old woman is friendly, says 'hello' and, when asked if selling newspapers is her main job, replies straightforwardly that, no, it's only a very small part of her job, because she is an angel. At the expected dumbfounded response to this, the old woman describes how angels can be dressed as wrestlers, or building surveyors. They may have sweatbands on their wrists, carry plumb-lines in their hands, and even appear as grey-haired newspaper sellers with missing teeth: 'We don't always wear wings and haloes, you know.'

The angel tells the passenger that she has a message from God for him. She gives him an envelope with his name written on it and says that it contains the one thing he always forgets, and the one thing he needs to remember if he is going to get anywhere in life. The old woman then disappears. She's there one minute and gone the next, although the bus has not stopped or even slowed down. The passenger is then really scared that the angel is bringing judgment on him.

What does he always forget? he asks himself. Has it to do with prayers? Church? Has it to do with the person he keeps criticizing, or that habit he knows he has to kick? What is it that he always forgets? When he finally gets up the courage to open the envelope, he finds a white card. At first, he thinks it's empty of words. Then, when he turns it over, he sees that there are just four: 'I, God, love *you*.' The 'you' is underlined to remind him that this is the thing he always forgets—and the thing he needs to remember.[14] This indictment of our hectic 21st-century lifestyle, in which God is very easily forgotten, is a gentle and caring message so full of hope that it feels as if it has the power to change any life.

God's amazing love for us is being revealed every second of every day, even when, at times, there seems to be an element of necessary fatherly scrutiny. 'I tripped over an angel in the church porch one day,' said Terry, an Anglican priest and friend. 'He said, "Can I have a cup of tea?" and "What time is your service, because I want to stay?" He did stay, and everyone liked him, even though he looked a bit scruffy and smelled rather strong. He actually stayed through the next service, too. Then he said, "What's next?" I took him to the vicarage for lunch. Then he said he had to leave, so I gave him a lift to the next village. When we were nearly there, he said, "I need to walk now." I dropped him off. Then I looked through the mirror. He had disappeared, literally, into thin air! Back in church, people were saying, "He was definitely an angel. And he'd come to find out just how welcoming we are to strangers!"'

This mysterious young man was seen, in the most positive way, as being on a vital mission from God, which was fulfilled not only by his attendance at two church services but his acceptance of the food and drink so freely given. No wonder that one of Terry's favourite verses from the New Testament is from the letter to the

Hebrews: 'Let mutual love continue. Do not neglect to show hospitality to strangers, for by doing that some have entertained angels without knowing it' (Hebrews 13:1–2).

Conclusion

ANGELS EVERY DAY

Having studied the scriptures and spoken to many people who have experienced things they cannot logically explain, my conclusion is that angels do exist, and they are still used by God as his messengers and our guardians. He despatches them to minister to his children in times of special need, and to travel with those who are in danger or about to leave the only world they have ever known.

With Billy Graham and, long before him, the writers of Isaiah and Revelation, I also believe that angels ceaselessly worship before the throne of God in heaven. I heard with my own ears the angels singing after the death of my great-grandmother when I was ten years old.

I also believe, because the Bible tells me it, that angels will appear with Christ at the end of time to separate those who have followed his new commandment of love from those who have refused to acknowledge him. God's timing is different from ours—a thousand years are like one day in his sight (2 Peter 3:8). Jesus will return, bringing to glorious fulfilment Paul's vision in the first letter to the Thessalonians.

For the Lord himself, with a cry of command, with the archangel's call and with the sound of God's trumpet, will descend from heaven, and the dead in Christ will rise first. Then we who are alive, who are left, will be caught up in the clouds together with them to meet the Lord in the air; and so we will be with the Lord for ever. Therefore encourage one another with these words.

1 THESSALONIANS 4:16–18

None of this, though, answers the unavoidable question. Why did God send his angels to some people in the Bible and not others, who were just as worthy of messages and guardians, and in need of ministers and travelling companions? And if we are to believe the stories in other books, and those entrusted to me, why is he still singling out certain individuals for angelic attention and allowing the majority of us to muddle through on our own?

The answer is not simple. Many of the great biblical characters who met and spoke with angels were close to God and were prepared to follow him even when his requests seemed bizarre or impossible. Abraham and Moses are good examples of this, as are Mary the mother of Jesus, and the apostle Paul.

Contemporary accounts of angelic intervention are often preceded by the words, 'I prayed for help', yet there are occasions when prayers for help are not answered and rescuers never come. This seems to prove that the angels are agents of God's grace, and not ours to summon or command. It is important to include angels in our prayers, but not to view them as under our control, as if they can be conjured by magic.

There is a crucial 'health warning' to bear in mind when speaking of 'invoking' angelic powers. The Bible tells us categorically never to worship angels. Colossians 2:18 is emphatic on this point, and in Romans 1:24–25 we are solemnly warned against worshipping the creature rather than the creator. John, on the island of Patmos, gives a vivid word picture of how not to behave: 'Then I fell down at [the angel's] feet to worship him, but he said to me, "You must not do that! I am a fellow servant with you and your comrades who hold the testimony of Jesus. Worship God! For the testimony of Jesus is the spirit of prophecy"' (Revelation 19:10).

During my research for this book, I have met a woman for whom this warning is very relevant. Fascinated by the whole subject of angels, she decided to go on an 'angel workshop' weekend, which she saw advertised in a shop specializing in New Age paraphernalia. She came back very confused and distressed, describing strange ceremonies with smoke and circles, and invocations and prayers to

Michael and Gabriel. 'The thing that really upset me was that the name of Jesus was never mentioned,' she told me, adding firmly, 'I'd never go to anything like that again!'

Some of the stories related in this book deal with the very real sense, experienced by some people, of dead relatives 'coming back' as angels to take a dying person home to heaven. This again is an area of danger, because the scriptures warn us very clearly against trying to contact or communicate in any way with the dead (Leviticus 19:31). There is also no scriptural evidence of human beings 'becoming' angels after death.

I cannot state strongly enough that the Bible teaches us that all our worship should be directed towards God, whose face alone we should be seeking. However, being aware of his angels can enhance our times of praise and bring us closer to God. Many of their stories in scripture are thrilling and uplifting, and these stories can also be a source of great encouragement. Angels are a gift from God, if only we are open to their special and wonderful ministry.

Before his arrest and crucifixion, Jesus gave his disciples a new commandment: that they should love one another. 'Just as I have loved you, you also should love one another. By this everyone will know that you are my disciples, if you have love for one another' (John 13:34–35). If we, as 21st-century Christians, also follow this commandment, we can be 'angels' not only to other followers of Jesus but to the world at large. When we remember what angels actually do, it's not too difficult to imagine an everyday scenario where we might bring the good news of companionship to someone in our neighbourhood who is lonely and isolated. We can stand up, like guardian angels, for those who are impoverished or otherwise exploited and abused in society. In recent years, many Christians have done just this by joining in protest marches, lobbying MPs or simply writing letters. We can be ministering angels to those who are ill or bereaved, sitting at bedsides, providing practical support as well as quiet hope that, through prayer and patience, life can again be good and maybe even more meaningful. We can also be a source of comfort and reassurance to a nervous traveller, providing a time of support and friendship that, though short, will probably never be forgotten.

It may seem confusing, or even offensive, for us as Christians to see angels being trivialized in gift shops or in the words of popular songs. But maybe God is even using angels there, to make people stop and think—just as Christmas carols piped into a shopping mall might have an evangelistic effect.

Finally, I think it's important never to forget that past generations had a different attitude to angels. We see it in Victorian cemeteries, where stone and marble angels still stand guard over the resting places of our ancestors, but we also hear it in the childhood prayers remembered by elderly people. 'When I was a small child, I was taught the following prayer,' writes Irene, a dear friend who is now over 90. 'More than 85 years on, I still use it every night.'

Lord, keep us safe this night,
Secure from all our fears,
May angels guide us while we sleep
Till morning light appears. Amen.

Similar childhood prayers are possibly still rising, night after night, from all over the world, ascending to God's throne where his worshipping messengers, guardians, ministers and travelling companions still wait, at his right hand, ready to do his bidding.

✜

NOTES

1   *Common Worship: Services and Prayers for the Church of England* (Church House Publishing, 2000), p. 441.

2   Hope Price, *Angels: True Stories of How They Touch Our Lives* (Pan Books, 1994), p. 41.

3   Joan Wester Anderson, *Where Angels Walk* (Hodder & Stoughton, 1995), p. 74.

4   Dr E.K. Victor Pearce, *Miracles and Angels* (Eagle, 1999), p. 123

5   Wallace and Mary Brown, *Angels on the Walls* (Kingsway, 2000), p. 39–40.

6   Pearce, *Miracles and Angels*, p. 39.

7   Pearce, *Miracles and Angels*, p. 26.

8   Billy Graham, *Angels: God's Secret Agents* (Hodder & Stoughton, 1995), p. 131.

9   *Common Worship*, p. 188.

10   *Common Worship*, p. 171.

11   Graham, *Angels*, p. 44.

12   Carol Hathorne, *Angels Keep Watch* (Christina Press, 1997), p. 11.

13   Price, *Angels*, p. 72.

14   John Bell, *He Was In the World* (Wild Goose Publications, 2004).

DREAM STORIES

A journey into the Bible's dreams and visions

RUSS PARKER

Dreams have fascinated humanity for thousands of years. In today's sceptical culture, we tend to dismiss dreams as having little or no importance, yet almost everybody has at least one dream they remember which may have had an effect upon them, sometimes lasting for many years.

In the Bible, dreams and visions were seen as powerful ways in which God communicated with his people. Prophets, early leaders of the Christian Church and rulers of foreign powers experienced dreams that had impact and consequence for the dreamer and those about him.

Dream Stories takes a look at how God spoke to his people through their dreams, from Jacob's dream at Bethel to Paul's night-time vision calling him to Macedonia. Russ Parker draws on twenty years' experience of pastoral ministry and examines these stories, showing how God still speaks to us through our dreams, bringing fresh opportunities for healing and growth.

ISBN 1 84101 072 3   £6.99
Available from your local Christian bookshop or, in case of difficulty, direct from BRF using the order form on page 125.

LIVING THE GOSPEL

The spirituality of St Francis and St Clare

HELEN JULIAN CSF

Finding freedom in simplicity and voluntary poverty, living in harmony with creation, seeking to be a brother to everyone and everything—so much of the teaching of St Francis directly challenges the values of today's consumer-driven culture, providing a radical, liberating alternative. Yet while he remains an enduringly popular figure in the history of Christian spirituality, St Clare, an early follower and teacher of his values, is far less well-known. *Living the Gospel* looks at St Francis and St Clare together, showing how they shared responsibility for the growth and influence of the Franciscan order, and how deeply rooted their teaching was in Scripture.

This book is ideal for people already interested in the teaching of St Francis as well as those whose explorations have extended no further than singing 'All creatures of our God and King'—a version of Francis' *Canticle of the Creatures*. And it introduces St Clare to a wider audience—a comparatively little-known but surprisingly influential female spiritual leader.

ISBN 1 84101 126 6   £5.99
Available from your local Christian bookshop or, in case of difficulty, direct from BRF using the order form on page 125.

ORDER FORM

REF	TITLE	PRICE	QTY	TOTAL
072 3	*Dream Stories*	£6.99		
126 6	*Living the Gospel*	£5.99		

POSTAGE AND PACKING CHARGES						
order value	UK	Europe	Surface	Air Mail	Postage and packing:	
£7.00 & under	£1.25	£3.00	£3.50	£5.50	Donation:	
£7.01–£30.00	£2.25	£5.50	£6.50	£10.00	**Total enclosed:**	
Over £30.00	free	prices on request				

Name _____ Account Number _____

Address _____

_____ Postcode _____

Telephone Number _____ Email _____

Payment by: ☐ Cheque ☐ Mastercard ☐ Visa ☐ Postal Order ☐ Switch

Card no. ☐☐☐☐ ☐☐☐☐ ☐☐☐☐ ☐☐☐☐

Expires ☐☐ ☐☐   Issue no. of Switch card ☐☐☐

Signature _____ Date _____

All orders must be accompanied by the appropriate payment.

Please send your completed order form to:
BRF, First Floor, Elsfield Hall, 15–17 Elsfield Way, Oxford OX2 8FG
Tel. 01865 319700 / Fax. 01865 319701 Email: enquiries@brf.org.uk

☐ Please send me further information about BRF publications.

Available from your local Christian bookshop.   BRF is a Registered Charity

Resourcing your spiritual journey

through...

- Bible reading notes
- Books for Advent & Lent
- Books for Bible study and prayer
- Books to resource those working with under 11s in school, church and at home

- Quiet days and retreats
- Training for primary teachers and children's leaders
- Godly Play
- Barnabas Live

For more information, visit the **brf** website at **www.brf.org.uk**